TRAUMA IN THE LIVES OF CHILDREN

....

About the Author

Kendall Johnson was born in Pomona, California, in 1945, the son of a college professor and an elementary school teacher. After completing high school he attended the California Polytechnic Institute in Pomona to study social sciences. In 1965 he joined the Navy and served for a time in Vietnam. Upon his return he started work as a psychiatric technician, married and resumed college studies. Over the next ten years, he obtained master's degrees in philosophy, counseling, and education, and a doctoral degree in Clinical Psychology.

Dr. Johnson's publications include papers on divorce mediation and child custody, crisis management in schools, and family sculpture, a group intervention strategy. After receiving training in Critical Incident Stress Debriefing he adapted the techniques for a school setting. This became the subject of a booklet published in 1987 titled *Classroom Crisis: A Readi-Reference Guide.* He is now writing a workbook for traumatized adolescents, and a resource booklet for disaster planners.

Currently, Dr. Johnson is a mentor teacher in a school for troubled teens and maintains a private practice as a family therapist. He regularly delivers seminars on crisis management, the effects of trauma on children, and teacher trauma and self care to school personnel, mental health professionals, and emergency care givers. He is an adjunct faculty member of the California Specialized Training Institute (Governor's Office of Emergency Services), a Professional Advisory Board member of the Center for Study of Psychological Trauma, Los Angeles, and a critical stress adviser to the National Fire Protection Association.

Kendall Johnson and his wife Wendy Losh live in Claremont, California. They have two children, a son Trevor and a daughter, Whitney.

TRAUMA IN THE LIVES OF CHILDREN

Crisis and Stress Management
Techniques for Teachers, Counselors,
and Student Service Professionals

Kendall Johnson, Ph.D.

First U.S. edition published in 1989 by Hunter House Inc.,
Publishers

Hunter House Inc.
P.O. Box 847
Claremont, CA 91711.

Library of Congress Cataloging-in-Publication Data:

Johnson, Kendall, 1945–
    Trauma in the lives of children.

    Bibliography: p.
    Includes index.
    1. Stress in children. 2. Post-traumatic stress disorder in
children. I. Title.
RJ507.S77J64   1989   155.4   88–32037
ISBN 0-89793-055-X
ISBN 0-89793-056-8 (pbk.)

Book design by Qalagraphia
Cover design by Teri Robertson
Line art by Renee Krikken
Copy editing by Judy Selhorst
Editorial manager: Jennifer D. Trzyna
Production manager: Paul J. Frindt
Set in Times Roman by 847 Communications, Claremont, CA
Printed by Edwards Bros., Inc., Ann Arbor, MI
Manufactured in the United States of America

TABLE OF CONTENTS

ACKNOWLEDGMENTS

It is said that all wars are won first on the home front, and that is indeed the case with books. No book is probably important enough to warrant the time, anguish, expense, and psychological absence that it inflicts upon family life. Yet visionaries persist and families endure.

Thus heartfelt thanks are due first to my wife, Wendy Losh, who never faltered in her support of this project. Wendy has always been a resonant sounding board for new ideas (after all, she is a musician), and she has time and again provided me with wise editorial advice. Our relationship has always been premised upon the idea that if something needed to be said or written, it had to be, and she has brought a fresh and compassionate perspective to our mutual interest in human behavior.

I owe a tremendous debt of gratitude to Dr. Jeffrey Mitchell of the Department of Emergency Health Services, University of Maryland. Jeff has provided me both direction and encouragement in this endeavor. More importantly perhaps, I have found his sense of mission highly infectious. Like this book, Jeff's work is devoted to easing human suffering.

Warm thanks are due to Spencer Eth, M.D. of the Brentwood V.A. Hospital, University of California, Los Angles, and the Center for the Study of Psychological Trauma. I am honored by Dr. Eth's input, as his research and leadership at the Center have been groundbreaking in the field of pediatric psychotraumatology.

Finally, I must acknowledge the help I've received from Hunter House. To Judy Selhorst, I extend my thanks for her keen editorial work. To Paul Frindt, my deep respect for his production wizardry. And finally, to publisher Kiran Rana, my appreciation and gratitude for his creativity and willingness to work with me to bring an unformed and unruly manuscript to completion.

Kendall Johnson
Claremont, 1989

DEDICATION

This book is dedicated to my son Trevor Losh-Johnson,
and to my daughter Whitney Losh-Johnson, in fervent
hopes that it never applies to them. If it does, however, I
hope with equal fervency that the adults around them at
that time possess the awareness and skills this book offers.

FOREWORD

CHILDREN TOUCH OUR LIVES, bring us joy, stir our souls. We cherish them as a delicate resource and a hope for a better tomorrow. Adults attempt to provide an environment that encourages their growth and gives them the courage necessary to improve the world. Adults do freely for children what they would resist vigorously if asked to do for other adults. They protect children, care for them, love them, and place hopes and dreams upon them.

Parents' and teachers' best attempts to provide a safe, uncomplicated environment for children is no fail-safe insurance policy against the traumas and distortions of human life. Unfortunately, some adults even participate knowingly and actively in self-serving destructive behaviors that leave the lives of children in chaos. Children, despite the very best efforts to protect them, are used in a wide assortment of dangerous, illegal, and destructive endeavors to satisfy the petty needs of adults. Children are cheated, sexually abused, neglected, ignored, injured, and even killed so that adults might be satisfied.

In addition, children face the same traumatic events that affect the lives of adults all around them. They become ill, experience accidents, and are exposed to fires and other disasters. Being a child offers no protection against loss, grief, or other emotional traumas. Neither does it protect them from illness, accidents, or death. Disturbing events in their own families, in the lives of their friends, or in the world may leave children feeling confused, uncertain, and frightened. Their self-esteem is frequently damaged as a result of traumatic experiences, and they may seek relief and reassurance in drugs. Under severe circumstances, children may try to escape the turmoil of their lives by running away or, even more tragically, in suicide. Children can be victims many times over before they reach adulthood.

Parents and teachers are frequently bewildered when faced with a traumatized child or group of distressed children. They turn anxiously toward health care professionals and psychological support services, only to find that specialists are frequently not adequately trained, skilled, or experienced to offer sound advice on how best to help damaged children. Research in libraries may be no more reassuring, because the existing literature on trauma in the lives of children is quite sparse; the literature that is available is usually not useful when applied to the real-life situations many children are facing.

Trauma in the Lives of Children needed to be written. It fills a serious gap in the literature on children. It provides teachers, school psychologists, health care professionals, mental health workers, and parents with practical information they might immediately apply to distressed children to relieve their pain. It explores the causes and effects of pediatric and adolescent emotional trauma. The information contained in this book will help adults, so they do not have to stand idle while children suffer. *Trauma in the Lives of Children* gives adults power to initiate changes in the care of children before the effects of traumatic events have the opportunity to become entrenched. The book provides information on the latest intervention strategies being employed in many areas of the country. These strategies have been designed to reduce the impact of traumatic events on children and to restore to children the happiest and most growth-enhancing circumstances possible in their schools and in their homes.

The author of this book, Kendall Johnson, has demonstrated consistent deep concern for children, both as a teacher and more recently as a mental health professional. He has spent considerable energy researching trauma and its effects on people. Dr. Johnson holds a Ph.D. in clinical psychology and serves as a consultant for California school districts and other organizations. He specializes in stress and crisis management as well as child sexual abuse and chemical dependency in children. He offers much to the field of child and adolescent development, and *Trauma in the Lives of Children* is another valuable contribution, devoted to the care of children after they have been exposed to the more painful aspects of life.

Jeffrey T. Mitchell, Ph.D.

Assistant Professor of Emergency Health Services
University of Maryland, Baltimore County Campus

PREFACE

SOCIETY GENERALLY VIEWS CHILDHOOD as a naturally happy time, free of responsibilities and worries. But the implication that children are somehow protected from the emotional effects of traumatic events is tragically false. All of us face the possibility of a disaster striking at any moment. A major earthquake, a plane crash, a fire, or a terrorist attack may be occurring as you read these words. Children are, in fact, as susceptible to trauma as adults, even though their suffering is commonly overlooked. Since the Second World War, mental health professionals have begun to recognize the dire consequences that can follow calamitous events. The first children studied were the survivors of the Nazi concentration camps. Many of these youngsters remained chronically frightened, depressed, and tormented. Today we find strikingly similar symptoms in Southeast Asian and Central American refugee children who have experienced war, confinement, and separation from their families.

American children have also encountered a series of catastrophes. In 1972, a flood washed away a West Virginia mining town. The displaced children reported a variety of persistent psychological and physical complaints. More recent studies of natural and human-induced disasters confirm severe distress in the child victims and serve to remind us that parents may be quite unaware of the extent of their own children's discomfort. My own work has centered on young witnesses of lethal violence. Each year in the United States more than 20,000 homicides are committed, often in the presence of the children of the deceased. The vast majority of these child witnesses develop the psychiatric syndrome of Posttraumatic Stress Disorder and are plagued by painful, intrusive memories, personality alterations, school difficulties, and behavioral disturbances. Although these children have usually escaped physical injury, in every case emotional wounds are the inevitable legacy of their exposure to violence.

Trauma in the Lives of Children confronts the neglect that traumatized youngsters have suffered for so long. In the pages that follow we are first introduced to the pathologic elements of crises that produce psychiatric symptoms. Identification of traumatic situations is a necessary first step in organizing a therapeutic intervention. We then learn of the spectrum of responses found in children and adolescents exposed to crisis. Several useful tables summarize the key signs and developmental features of Posttraumatic Stress Disorder. This term, PTSD, first appeared in the third edition of the American Psychiatric Association's *Diagnostic and Statistical Manual* (DSM-III) in 1980, and has become emblematic of the agony associated with Vietnam veterans, rape victims, and other disaster survivors. However, children are barely mentioned in the PTSD section of the current revision of DSM-III, an omission that underscores the value of this volume.

Ultimately, *Trauma in the Lives of Children* is about helping youngsters recover from overwhelming stress, and it contains a remarkable synthesis of useful techniques. Its view of children as embedded in a social context is instrumental in formulating a treatment plan. We see youth functioning in their families, schools, and communities, and see the subtle and dramatic effects that crises produce on these systems. This perspective naturally leads to a detailed exploration of strategies designed to assist traumatized children. The family, the school, and the therapist all have major and unique roles to play. Armed with the specific instructions found in later chapters, mental health professionals will be able to reverse the family's isolation and despair, to transform the classroom into an opportunity center for coping enhancement, and to empower themselves in their clinical encounters with traumatized children.

Trauma in the Lives of Children represents a sound foundation for the evolving field of pediatric psychotraumatology. By surveying the critical areas of concern, we also discover how much remains to be accomplished, especially with regard to primary prevention. Ideally, we would like to protect our environment from the ravages of disaster, or at least immunize our children from their devastating effects. So far we have not been successful in achieving either. But as this book so well documents, we can offer effective help to our young patients, their families, and their schools in the aftermath of trauma. This work must be given priority attention both because of the prevalence of PTSD and because of its responsiveness to therapeutic intervention. Dr. Kendall Johnson, master teacher and therapist, is to be congratulated on an important contribution to the mental health literature. *Trauma in the Lives of Children* deserves to be read by every professional who cares for children in our troubled world.

Spencer Eth, M.D.

Associate Chief of Psychiatry
Veterans Administration Medical Center
West Los Angeles, California

INTRODUCTION

TRAUMA: CONTEXT AND CONCERNS

> Residents of a quiet community near Wichita, Kansas, were stunned when a fourteen-year-old junior high student took an M-1 rifle and a .375 caliber Magnum pistol to school and opened fire in a main hallway. The shots killed the school's popular thirty-five-year-old principal and wounded two teachers and a student.
>
> *Safe Schools and Quality Schooling, 1988*
> (National School Safety Center pamphlet)

OVER THE PAST FEW YEARS the public has been inundated with reports of trauma in the lives of children. Combining concern for children with a morbid and sometimes tasteless fascination, the media rush to the scene of crisis after crisis, and viewers are treated to weekly dramas involving all sorts of catastrophes. And the world obliges. Teachers all over the country were stunned to see the space shuttle *Challenger* explode while their students watched in horror. In Whittier, California, an entire school district was swamped with requests for counseling from parents of distraught children who had been near the epicenter of the major October 1987 earthquake. Earlier that year, a twelve-year-old Missouri student who had been the victim of repeated bullying fatally shot another student and then committed suicide.

Social scientists, too, provide more accurate information every day regarding the prevalence of sexual crimes against children. Researchers compile frequency statistics and writers consolidate these studies into a wide assortment of books that range from theoretical dissertations to how-to-cope guides. Legislators respond to the public outrage with various types of legislation and

1

funding for research projects, educational programs, and treatment facilities. All of this awareness and concern is, basically, good for children.

Professionals who work with children, however, greet the media coverage with mixed feelings. They recognize the value of public awareness and welcome the researchers and new programs now becoming available. They have committed their professional lives to the well-being of children, and they know that this new help is badly needed. Yet with the fervor comes new pressure. Much of the legislation creates new liabilities for child-care professionals—liabilities that can be severe. There is much to fear from a lawsuit for either overreacting or underreacting in child abuse situations, an area in which the law is still complex and vague. With today's media hungry for news about children's traumas, a professional's reputation can be shattered by one false accusation.

In addition, many professionals who work with children are not trained to manage crisis situations involving those children. Teachers are rarely given any training in what to do during or following classroom crises. Most school districts provide little more than first aid drill and fire drill procedures. The training of therapists and social workers occasionally covers the *effects* of crisis but rarely includes training in crisis intervention. Program administrators normally receive no training in trauma work unless as a part of early training. Yet, each of these professionals either supervises someone who could be confronted by a child in real distress or may personally be called upon to deal with such a child. With little or no training in crisis management and with increased legal and social pressure to handle such incidents properly, professionals need solid information about trauma in the lives of children, with an emphasis upon practical aspects of crisis management.

Of particular concern is the increased need for interagency, interdisciplinary contact. In the school situation, teachers and administrators may be the first professionals aware of a child's trauma and the ones who maintain continuity of contact with the child over the course of the posttraumatic reaction. They are often in the best position to determine when to refer the child for specialized help. Yet, for most teachers and administrators, therapy is a black box, the workings of which they do not understand. They lack a knowledge of when referral is appropriate and why it should be made. Further, while they are in the position to provide useful "real-time" information regarding the child's recent behavioral changes, they frequently do not know (or feel they do not know) what information is relevant to therapists.

Therapists, social workers, and other mental health professionals often find themselves in a similar position. Although they are more familiar with school procedures and routines, they frequently do not know what to look for or what to recommend to schools when serving in a consulting capacity. With public exposure motivating schools to become more proactive in meeting children's posttraumatic needs, mental health professionals are increasingly called upon to provide consultation and assistance in crisis situations.

What happens to a child following a crisis? How might adults best respond to children in crisis to help them cut their losses? When is an incident psychologically critical? Counselors, teachers, and medical staff—anyone who works with children professionally—need to know the answers to these questions in order to intervene effectively. How do crises affect younger children differently than older children? What are the effects of background differences? Are there commonalities in response to crisis? What should one look for in identifying delayed reactions to crisis?

The answers to these and many related questions prove valuable for the professional when he or she is called upon to

— identify crisis situations;
— recognize who is and who is not affected;
— decide who is at risk in a given situation;
— formulate options;
— intervene appropriately;
— monitor postcrisis recovery; and
— determine when and how to follow up.

The aim of this book is to address and answer these questions for teachers, administrators, counselors, psychologists, therapists, social workers, concerned parents, and others who work with, care for, or provide services to children. Because the audience is broad and the needs of different groups in the audience vary so widely, the chapters also vary in terms of content, style, and tone. Following is a brief synopsis of each chapter.

Chapter I investigates current research regarding crises. Providing general background information, "What We Know About Crisis" reviews and summarizes two types of studies. First, key reports that outline basic facts regarding trauma are presented. For purposes of review, children's traumatic events are classified into three groups: victimization, loss, and family pathology. The dynamics of each group are discussed in general, and then a representative example is presented in greater detail for illustration. This approach provides readers with the background information necessary for the management of such events. Chapter I is largely descriptive, outlining the role played by traumatic events in children's lives.

Adolescent crises are discussed separately in this chapter. The various types of adolescent maladaptive behaviors, such as substance abuse, running away, or self-destructive activities, are often reactions to prior traumas that create current crises as well. The resulting interactive effects of prior trauma and present individual and family crises due to adolescent acting out create unique problems. Because these situations so complicate the work of professionals, they need to be viewed separately from the general discussion of crises.

Chapter II, "Children's Reactions to Trauma," begins by describing children's acute, situational reactions to crisis situations. One child's excitement may be another's trauma, and this can create identification problems for professionals. Emotional, physical, and behavioral signs of distress during or just after a crisis are detailed in this chapter to increase the professional's ability to discern when a child is showing a traumatic reaction.

The concept of Posttraumatic Stress Disorder (PTSD) explains the delayed reactions children display toward crisis. Chapter II reviews current studies outlining the signs and symptoms of posttraumatic stress response in children. How this delayed response functions and the manner in which it manifests in the lives of traumatized children are explored to aid in increasing professional awareness and crisis management skills. Finally, the fascinating developmental implications of childhood trauma are discussed.

Chapter III, "What the Schools Can Do," outlines the helpful, healthful steps school personnel can take in managing children's crises. Outside of the family, schools are by far the most influential institutions shaping children's lives. Because children normally spend a great amount of time in school, it may be considered a naturalistic setting compared to the clinician's office. Schools provide a potentially healing or hurtful environment for children who have been traumatized, depending upon the organizational climate and staff expertise. Because school personnel are leery of being accused of "doing therapy," which would be beyond their scope of practice, they sometimes ignore the very real and important role they can play in children's lives by creating a therapeutic context. Helping children to grow emotionally is clearly within the educator's scope of activity. Chapter III explores the many ways educators can interact with the traumatized child, allowing the natural healing process to take place. Toward this end, guidelines for individual conferencing are provided. Additionally, and unique to this book, classroom debriefings are discussed. Critical incidents frequently occur that affect an entire group. These events may either strengthen or weaken class cohesiveness, depending in large part upon how they are handled. Class debriefings are presented as a crisis management strategy, designed to maintain and strengthen class cohesiveness following an incident affecting the entire class.

This discussion of crisis management strategies in the school will be of particular benefit to mental health professionals. Increasingly, therapists, social workers, and other mental health professionals are being called into school postcrisis situations to provide consultation or direct intervention. Often these professionals are not familiar with school organization or practice and need practical guidelines to augment their theoretical knowledge. Chapter III presents directions, approaches, and strategies for providing effective assistance.

Chapter IV, "What Therapists Can Do," discusses how therapists can help traumatized children within a clinical setting. While a single chapter cannot provide a comprehensive discussion of treatment, this chapter presents a meaningful overview that will be useful to both therapists and nontherapists on several counts. While therapists have access to detailed literature about treatment modalities and outcomes, a general overview can address the central clinical task. Consideration of core therapeutic issues and direction is invaluable for coordinating the therapist's skills and resources with the traumatized child's needs.

Nontherapists, who are not familiar with the conventions and methodology of therapeutic intervention, are often unclear about where and when to refer. They are often not good consumers of therapy because they have no understanding of what the various approaches have to offer. Because they frequently do not know what the child can expect, they cannot help prepare the child for or assess the progress of treatment. Finally, nontherapists do not know which of their observations or impressions might be valuable, nor do they know what sorts of questions to ask. Many nontherapists make referrals to therapy and then just hope for the best.

One of the strengths of this book is that it can provide nontherapists with a common ground, a translation of the direction, methods, and reasons behind posttrauma therapy. Accordingly, Chapter IV describes the therapeutic task in treating posttrauma cases, beginning with on-scene crisis intervention. Following the discussion of acute, situational treatment, the longer-term treatment of posttrauma disorders is explored. This focuses upon the major therapeutic "kernel" of the reexperiencing, releasing, and reintegrating of traumatic experience. And because adolescents, always a class by themselves, raise treatment issues that require additional discussion, the chapter describes family mediation as an adjunct technique useful in posttrauma adolescent treatment.

It is nearly impossible to deal with children in crisis without dealing with their families as well. At the very least this involves notifications, progress reports, or information queries by phone. More often, it entails discussion in which observations and resources are shared and problem solving occurs. In extreme cases, professionals may be "triangled" into conflictual or hopeless/helpless family situations in which they are either blamed for the difficulties or expected to solve them. Crisis affects families deeply and can create chaotic change. Whether the child's trauma occurs outside the family or within it, the family as a whole will be affected, and so, of course, will the task of the professional.

Thus Chapter V, "Families in Crisis," investigates the ways in which families react to crisis situations and their aftereffects. Beginning with the distinction between the process and content dimensions of family functioning, the chapter shows how those dynamics can affect the helping professional. Several critical dimensions are described and illustrated, with an emphasis upon the way they can present pitfalls for professionals. Pathological family functioning is outlined using the same critical dynamics as organizing principles. A three-stage model of family adaptation to crisis shows how crisis can serve to strengthen or disturb family relationships. Finally, an informal troubleshooting guide provides the assessment information regarding family health and stage of crisis response that professionals need to guide their interaction with the family.

Chapter VI, "Toward Prevention," discusses the various elements of crisis prevention. The basic premise of this book is that while crises themselves can never be eliminated, their effects can be softened significantly by effective intervention. Parents and teachers cannot keep airplanes from falling out of the sky, or prevent grandparents from dying, but well-planned interventions can prepare children (and adults) for crises, thereby moderating their effects. This chapter explores some basic types of precrisis intervention that can go far in decreasing the harmful effects critical incidents can create.

First, children can be exposed to learning experiences designed to make them more stress resilient. Children need to be aware of their own feeling states and those of others so that they can communicate their feelings and needs; they need to have access to viable support systems, to know how to solve problems and make decisions, and to have a basically solid sense of self-esteem.

Second, children can be given trauma-specific instruction. Much of the difficulty with critical incidents comes from a sense of isolation and the compounding effect of secondary reactions. Children need to know the range of critical incidents; they need to learn what can be done about them and then face the fact that such incidents do, in fact, occur to people. When children do not know what reactions they are likely to have following a trauma, those effects may result in greater fear and disorientation. Finally, staff members are in the similar position of needing knowledge about their own stress reactions under such circumstances.

Thus Chapter VI discusses the general elements of stress management, communication, support systems, and problem-solving and decision-making skills, and also outlines appropriate trauma-specific education. The contextual background of professional stress is discussed, as well as staff stress reactions to critical incidents. This diverse range of subjects, taken together under the broad rubric of prevention, provides the elements of a proactive program.

Several loose ends are tied up in Appendix I and Appendix II. While much has been said relating specific childhood traumas to specific forms of adolescent acting out, the general developmental connection has received very little empirical support. In addition, the actual outcome of different intervention behaviors has received little if any empirical verification. Accordingly, Appendix I reports original research addressing both the relationship between childhood traumas and subsequent adolescent development and the results of the style of intervention in terms of long-range effects. The results support the developmental connection between traumas and subsequent difficulties and clearly show five distinct interactional styles that have moderating or compounding effects on the behavioral outcome. This is exciting in that it provides empirical justification for setting directions in crisis management. This report is edited somewhat, as much of the literature and discussion appear elsewhere in the book.

Appendix II is a resource guide for professionals. The suggestions given and the agencies listed include sources of information, support, and referral.

The purpose of this book is to increase the understanding of children's trauma and provide directions for the management of such crises. The book attempts to cross disciplinary lines and suggest helping strategies that focus and coordinate the work of both school and clinic. It is hoped that school personnel will explore the therapy chapter and that clinicians will familiarize themselves with the discussion on school intervention. Greater orchestration of posttrauma care is possible and sorely needed. It is further hoped that parents will investigate each chapter, so that they will know not only what to do, but what to expect of professionals in the event of trauma in the lives of their children.

CHAPTER I

WHAT WE KNOW ABOUT CRISIS

> In a recent study conducted by the Fullerton, California, Police Department, leading discipline problems of the 1940s were contrasted with the 1980s. In the 40s, teachers were confronted with gum chewing, walking out of line, talking, and not using wastebaskets. In the 1980s, schools face substance abuse, gangs, robbery, arson, and bombings.
>
> *Safe Schools and Quality Schooling, 1988*
> (National School Safety Center pamphlet)

OVERVIEW

Every professional dealing with children or their families needs to have an awareness of the types and frequencies of childhood traumas. Further, the manner in which adolescent crises are both a product of prior childhood traumas and also a compounding present crisis must be understood. This chapter presents basic background information concerning childhood and adolescent crises. Studies of the effects of victimization, loss, and dysfunctional families are reviewed, as are the various major maladaptive behaviors of adolescents.

CHAPTER CONTENTS:

CHILDHOOD TRAUMAS
Victimization—Loss—Family Pathology

ADOLESCENT CRISES AND MALADAPTIVE BEHAVIORS
Suicide—Runaways—Serious School Attendance Problems—Drug and Alcohol Abuse

CONCLUSION

THIS CHAPTER PROVIDES A BRIEF REVIEW of current research studies in the area of childhood trauma. A comprehensive review of all the research currently available or being done in this area is beyond the scope of this book, but a representative summary, suggestive and directive rather than exhaustive, is presented here. General background information is provided for those new to the field and, for those more familiar with the territory, resources for further reading and research are suggested.

CHILDHOOD TRAUMAS

The kinds of experiences or conditions that can seriously hurt children are legion. For purposes of review here, they are classified into three groups: victimization, loss, and family pathology. In this chapter, each group is discussed in turn. An investigation of the common characteristics among the various types of incidents within the group is presented, and then a representative example is discussed in greater detail.

VICTIMIZATION

Under the category of victimization can be included assault, robbery, rape, incest, and serious accidents. Because incest, unlike the others, tends to be a long-term problem and a manifestation of serious family pathology, it could also be considered under the section on family pathology.

Bard and Sangrey (1979), in their theoretical discussion of victimization, identify three stages through which victims of crime tend to pass: impact, recoil, and reorganization. Their work is particularly relevant to this review because the reaction patterns they identify can be generalized to other types of victimization.

Impact

Victimization experiences tend to be of high intensity and short duration. Consequently, the first stage of reaction includes emotional shock symptoms such as numbness and feelings of vulnerability and helplessness. Lindemann (1944) identified the following somatic symptoms:

1. tightness in the throat

2. choking and shortness of breath

3. an empty feeling in the abdomen

4. lack of muscle power

Bard and Sangrey add the following to this list, treating the reaction to victimization as an acute grief reaction:

5. sleep disturbances

6. loss of appetite

Other symptoms may manifest during this period. Victims often feel shame and guilt concerning their state, blaming themselves for the ordeal. Lerner (1970) postulates a "just world" theory that may account for this reaction. In brief, the theory states that it is normal to believe that the world is rational and that consequences are in accordance with justice. Thus a person who is victimized might logically conclude that he or she must have deserved it somehow.

Recoil

The recoil stage consists of the individual's attempts to deal emotionally with the victimizing event. Most individuals alternate between trying to go on with their lives as though the event never happened and returning periodically and almost obsessively to the event and its ramifications. The obsessional phases include compensatory fantasies and planning and, often, phobic reactions. This pattern of behavior seems to represent cognitive attempts at regaining equilibrium. In addition, probably as a further attempt to compensate for damage to the self or to provide enough cognitive coherence to allow them to cope, victims in the recoil phase frequently experience problems of blaming. Besides blaming themselves, victims sometimes blame friends, family, or police (Bard & Sangrey, 1979).

Reorganization

The third and final stage of response to victimization is characterized by a return to psychological equilibrium. Obsessional fear and anger become modulated, though there are occasional flashbacks or extreme agitation. While recovery depends upon many factors (such as prior traumas, support, and extent of violation), the victim in the reorganization phase is able to focus upon life-enhancing activities rather than simply coping.

The Effects of Sexual Abuse

Sexual abuse victims have reported depression, guilt, poor self-esteem, and feelings of inferiority in later life (Courtois, 1979; Herman, 1981). Interpersonal problems such as isolation, alienation, and distrust (Courtois, 1979), fear of men (Herman, 1981), transient and/or negative relationships (Herman, 1981), repeat victimization (Briere, 1984), promiscuity (Courtois, 1979), and sexual dysfunction (Kaplan, 1979) have also been associated with childhood sexual victimization.

Of the few studies that included nonclinical samples, two focused upon the long-term effects of childhood sexual abuse—those conducted by Tsai, Feldman-Summers, and Edgar (1979) and Briere and Runtz (1985). Tsai et al. compared psychotherapy clients with reported sexually abusive backgrounds to women in the general population with and without sexually abusive backgrounds. On the basis of MMPI scores, they concluded that sexual abuse need not produce long-term effects and related positive outcomes to mediating aspects of the situation itself.

In their 1985 study, Briere and Runtz included a nonclinical abused group and used more appropriate instrumentation to measure postabuse trauma (symptom checklists). Their results showed significant long-term symptomatology associated with a history of sexual child abuse among nonclinical adult women.

They report that 15% of 278 university women had sexual contact with an older person prior to age 15. These women reported higher levels of dissociation, somatization, anxiety, and depression than did nonabused women. Briere and Runtz speculate that dissociation may initially function as a coping strategy and then later become an autonomous symptom. Anxiety and depression, they argue, appear to be conditioned or secondary learned responses to the sexual abuse, persisting into later life in a manner similar to unresolved rape trauma (Burgess & Holstrom, 1974). In addition,

Briere and Runtz correlate abuse-related symptomatology with factors associated with the abusive incident such as perpetrator age, total number of perpetrators, use of force, parental incest, completed intercourse, and duration of abuse.

Reviewing clinical studies, Green (1985) concludes that despite methodological problems in the research, symptoms manifested by incest victims resemble those found in rape victims by Burgess and Holstrom (1974), including fear, sleep and eating disturbances, guilt, decreased or constricted levels of general functioning, sexual problems, and irritability.

Green (1985) presents three case studies of incest victims, ranging in age from 18 months to 28 years. Their symptoms included the following:

1. fear, startle reactions, and anxiety

2. repetition, reenactment, or flashback to the trauma

3. sleep disturbance and other depressive phenomena, including excessive guilt

4. ego constriction or regression

5. explosive and maladaptive expressions of anger (p. 161)

LOSS

Literature related to loss generally focuses upon specific losses. These can be classified as apparent losses, losses as a part of change, and unnoticed loss (Frears & Schneider, 1981). Apparent losses include major losses that are obvious, resulting from such events as death of a relative or friend, permanent and involuntary separation, illness, or injury. Other losses are less dramatic and occur as a normal part of life changes. These can include divorce, moving, changing schools, or other significant changes in the environment, as well as leaving home, weaning, puberty, and aging. Finally, some losses are not normally identified as such but nevertheless trigger loss responses in many people. These are often difficult to deal with as they do not trigger normal social supports in the same manner as recognizable loss. Unnoticed losses can include marriage or remarriage, achievements, success, and growth.

Although these changes are usually considered to be positive, they do represent the loss of an earlier life-style and coping pattern. Such a loss can create turmoil even though the overall life change is for the good.

The adjustment to loss requires an elaborate process whereby the subject gradually, in stages, accommodates to the changed reality. The process of bereavement has been outlined by Kübler-Ross (1969) as following the five major stages of denial, anger, bargaining, depression, and acceptance (1969); these stages seem to apply to other losses as well. However, Frears and Schneider (1981) present a more elaborate six-stage model:

1. initial awareness (including shock, loss of equilibrium, and lowered resistance to infection)

2. strategies to overcome loss (including adaptive defense cycles of holding on and letting go)

3. awareness of loss (including exploration of extent of loss and its ramifications, such as loneliness, helplessness, and exhaustion)

4. completions (healing, acceptance, and resolution, freeing the energy invested in the loss)

5. empowering the self (in areas that were out of balance prior to the loss)

6. transcending the loss (growth following completions and re-balancing)

Children under ten years of age have not yet developed the capacity to recognize, understand, and resolve loss. Not only are they likely to make incorrect assumptions regarding the loss, but their dependent role and lack of ability to remove themselves from unbearable situations render them vulnerable to special problems. When loss affects the family, children may develop apathy and withdrawal behaviors because their basic needs are not being met during the parents' own grieving. Young children are not adept at limiting their helplessness (awareness) or resolving their loss (completions) (Frears & Schneider, 1981).

An appreciation of the development of the concept of death

is central to understanding children's reactions to loss. Wass (1984) discusses this development from a Piagetian perspective; his correlation of predominant death concepts with stages of cognitive development is presented in Table 1.

Wass and Cason (1984) further discuss these phase-correlated death concepts in terms of the types of fears and anxieties associated with them. During the sensorimotor stage death is not conceptualized and responses to death are simply responses to the immediate loss.

Preoperational-stage children, however, conceive of death as a temporary, reversible state, caused phenomenologically (that is, caused by whatever appears immediately preceding death), magically, or psychologically (in terms of motives). Hence their fears have to do with motivations, magical controls, and things they have come to associate with a death, as well as fears regarding magical controls and motivations. How a body is treated after death is of great concern to children at this stage, as death is not perceived to be an irreversible state. As a result, adults are often confused by the reactions to death of preoperational children.

During the concrete operations stage, children come to understand that death is irreversible. Causes of death are perceived to be external (such as violence, destruction, or accident). While anxiety related to the apparent capriciousness of death is lessened by this awareness, there is a focus upon postdeath decay. This preoccupation may be a means of coping with the dread that awareness of dying raises.

In adolescence there is the final development of the concepts of the personal and universal nature of death. The anxiety attendant upon this realization is somewhat contained, however, by the adolescent's ability to perceive death more as a personal threat in the very distant future.

The Case of Parental Death

These considerations regarding children's conceptions of death provide the background against which children's actual patterns of mourning take shape. On the basis of in-depth case analysis of 23 children of widely varying ages seen at a therapeutic school, Furman (1984) outlined basic elements of children's bereavement as a

Table 1: Development of Death Concepts

Life Period	Predominant Death Concepts
1. infancy	no concept of death
2. late infancy, early childhood	death is reversible; a temporary restriction, departure, or sleep
3. middle childhood, late or preadolescence	death is irreversible but capricious; external-internal physiological explanations
4. preadolescent, adolescent, adult	death is irreversible, universal, personal, but distant; natural, physiological, and theological explanations

Source: Wass (1984).

threefold task: (1) to understand and come to terms with the reality and circumstances of the death, (2) to mourn, and (3) to progress in the appropriate development of personality. This involves detachment (eventual resignation and withdrawal of emotional investment from what is no longer there) and identification (assimilation of attributes of the lost loved one).

Furman (1984) discusses how detachment and identification affect the process of adjustment to a new stepparent. After a certain length of time, once the child has detached significantly from the lost parent, he or she may choose a new parent substitute or redefine the relationship with the existing parent. If the parent remarries, however, this natural process is forced. Such a forced relationship is frequently experienced by the child as a violation of either an existing attachment to the lost parent or the child's internalized image of how a parent should be. In addition, unresolved mourning in children may lead them to avoid internalizing healthy attributes of the lost parent or to develop fears that they must avoid similar life decisions in order to avoid a similar fate.

Furman points out that the acute stage typically subsides after 6–18 months, but that it continues intermittently, triggered by anniversaries and developmental steps. Parent loss involves a loss of part of oneself and is experienced as diminution of self-worth and as isolation. Maladaptive coping with parent loss may take the form of intensifying detachment or increasing premature structuring.

Various authors have explored the relationship between specific significant losses during childhood and subsequent maladaptive behavior. In their review of the literature, Klagsbrun and Davis (1977) report that there is general agreement that a high correlation exists between substance abuse and parental loss. Bowlby (1961) indicates a high correlation between death of a parent and behavioral problems, particularly if the parent was lost prior to the child's reaching 5 years of age. Gregory (1965) correlates parental loss with delinquency and school attendance problems.

Such effects of parental loss upon subsequent development do not occur in a vacuum, however. Bowen (1978) states that "the intensity of the emotional reaction is governed by the functioning level of emotional integration of the family at the time, or by the functional importance to the family of the one who is lost" (p. 325).

Expanding upon this, Birchnell (1969) lists several factors that influence the degree of disruption the death causes:

1. the special relationship that existed between the lost parent and the child

2. the relationships that existed between the parent and the other family members

3. the controlling influence the parent exerted over other relationships within the family

4. the influences other family members exerted upon the relationship that existed between the child and the lost parent

5. the influence the child exerted upon the relationships that existed between the lost parent and the other family members (pp. 9–10)

FAMILY PATHOLOGY

The family, although greatly changed in terms of structure and values through the past thirty years, nevertheless remains a pervasive, formative force in children's development. Birchnell's discussion mentioned above illustrates this. Functioning as the primary learning milieu for individual behavior, the family provides the basic structure for children's values and expectations through their growth toward maturity (Satir, 1967). Consequently, families that show serious disturbance provide a faulty learning environment.

Coleman, Butcher, and Carson (1980) summarize the now burgeoning family dynamics literature into four broad categories of family dysfunction that lead to a high incidence of problems in child development and later psychopathology:

1. *Inadequate families:* These families lack the physical or psychological resources for coping with normal life stressors.

2. *Anti-social families:* These families have values that differ greatly from those of their communities in that they may encourage dishonesty, deceit, or other undesirable behaviors.

3. *Discordant and disturbed families:* These families may be characterized by fraudulent interpersonal contracts and disturbance (including fighting, gross irrationality, or enmeshment of the family in parental conflicts).

4. *Disrupted families:* These families have inadequately adjusted to the loss of family members through death, divorce, or separation.

These four categories have been found to be associated with higher incidences of psychological disorders leading to various maladaptive behaviors and to physical illness (Bloom, Asher, & White, 1978; Heatherington, Cox, & Cox, 1978; Langer & Michael, 1963; Lidz, Fleck, & Cornelison, 1965; Wolkind & Rutter, 1973).

Several specific patterns of parental influence appear regularly in the backgrounds of children showing emotional disturbances and faulty development. In their review, Coleman, et al. (1980) indicate the following patterns as pathogenic: rejection, overprotection, unrealistic demands, overpermissiveness, faulty discipline, inadequate and irrational communication, and undesirable parental models.

As illustration, Richman (1981) reports a series of studies conducted by himself and Rosenbaum investigating characteristics typical of the family at the time of a suicidal crisis in one of its members:

1. inability to accept necessary changes, including intolerance for separation, a symbiosis without empathy, and infantile fixations

2. role disturbances

3. affect disturbances, including one-sided handling of aggression and sexual difficulties with incestuous overtones

4. interpersonal difficulties, including reliance upon scapegoating, double-binding, and sadomasochistic relationships

5. close family system that is dominated by a fragile family member

6. communication disturbances

7. intolerance for crisis

The Case of Alcoholic Families

Whether alcoholism is or is not associated with genetic predisposition, studies of alcoholic families have shown that where one member is alcoholic, a dysfunctional pattern of interaction tends to emerge, affecting the children of the family to such an extent that subsequent maladaptive behaviors may be expected. Siegler, Osmond, and Newell (1968) describe the extreme manifestation of this pattern:

Alcoholism, like drug addiction and schizophrenia, is best seen as a form of family interaction in which one person is assigned the role of the "alcoholic" while the others play complementary roles, such as the martyred wife, the neglected children, the disgraced parents, and so forth. As this deadly game is played by mutual consent, any attempt to remove the key actor, the alcoholic, is bound to create difficulties for the other family members, who will attempt to restore their former game. (p. 579)

Family systems theorists view the family as an operational system and observe that change in the functioning of one family member is automatically followed by compensatory change in another family member (Bowen, 1978). They observe that children in alcoholic families evolve compensatory roles in reaction to dysfunctional parenting in order to maintain family cohesiveness and equilibrium.

Black (1979) describes three such children's roles:

1. *The Responsible One:* the child who provides structure for him- or herself and others within the often inconsistent home environment

2. *The Adjuster:* the child who compliantly adapts to the inconsistencies

3. *The Placater:* the child who helps others, possibly in response to guilt over family dysfunction

Black claims that "Responsible" children carry the need to control into their adult lives and frequently end up alone or in unmeaningful relationships; "Adjuster" children tend to grow up manipulated by others, suffer from low self-esteem, and end up inviting into their lives someone who has significant problems (frequently an alcoholic); "Placaters" grow up minimizing their own needs and subjugating them to those of others.

Wegscheider (1981) provides a similar description of this role differentiation, adding a fourth role to the list:

4. *The Troubled One:* the child who acts out the family problems, frequently getting into explicitly maladaptive behaviors

Thus the parental inconsistency, faulty communication, and

learned distrust common to alcoholic families force the children to adopt coping strategies that are often maladaptive.

SUMMARY

This review points out several similarities among experiences of victimization, loss, and pathogenic family structure in childhood. Each appears to create sufficient stress to cause behavioral symptomatology at the time of the experience, a finding that clearly has implications for involved professionals. When a crisis has occurred, sensitivity to the signs of trauma can help professionals determine whether or not particular children have been adversely affected by the event. In addition, this awareness can alert professionals to signs of trauma in children who have been in crisis prior to contact with the professional. These signs are discussed in detail in Chapter III.

All three of the conditions discussed in this chapter tend to result in similar patterns of subsequent maladaptive behavior in adolescence or adulthood, although it is not clear if different types of critical incidents predispose children to different specific maladaptive behaviors. This connection was given general support in the studies reviewed here, and Appendix I reports in detail the results of an independent study on this subject conducted by the author. The connection between critical incidents and maladaptive behaviors is of particular interest to those who work with troubled adolescents. As the next section points out, acting-out adolescents tend to report having experienced more trauma than do "normal" young people. This insight is especially useful to teachers, counselors, and medical staff dealing with youth. The practical implications of this finding for professionals are discussed in Chapter IV.

Finally, it appears that the degree of subsequent maladaptive response is moderated to some extent by various factors such as family or social support (Birchnell, 1969; Bowen,1978). The effects of different styles of adult interaction with children in crisis were also investigated in the study reported in Appendix I, and specific recommendations for dealing with such children grew out of that investigation; these are outlined and discussed in Chapter IV.

Concerned crisis management must be *aware* crisis management, and recommendations based on empirical data are of particular value to professionals confronted with children in crisis.

ADOLESCENT CRISES AND MALADAPTIVE BEHAVIORS

Why do the problems of young people seem so intense, so urgent? Those who work with adolescents in distress often remark that the crises seem to be more convoluted than those experienced by either younger children or adults. More often than not, young people's problems seem to become entangled with acting-out behavior, which complicates the work of any professional—therapeutic, medical, or educational—working with adolescents.

As these studies have indicated, children's traumas often result in maladaptive behavior later in adolescence. Thus, while adolescent crises are frequently situational (for example, loss), they are often compounded by the deleterious effects of acting out, which might include substance abuse or other self-destructive behavior. Professionals working with adolescents in crisis usually have to deal with elements of situational emergency, maladaptive behavioral patterns, and the residual effects of prior trauma in childhood.

Adolescence adds several dimensions to the general pattern of a child's response to crisis. First, the adolescent's conceptual abilities more closely resemble those of adults than they do those of younger children. Second, the emotional turmoil following adolescent developmental changes imparts a unique intensity to situational crises. Finally, adolescents usually have been through more prior traumas than younger children and bring with them certain special vulnerabilities.

While the previous section related a range of behavioral consequences in adolescence to certain specific critical incidents (CIs) in childhood, this section examines literature relating a range of antecedent critical incidents to specific maladaptive adolescent behaviors (MABs), including suicide, running away, serious school attendance problems, drug abuse, and alcohol abuse.

SUICIDE

Suicide is becoming an increasingly prevalent threat to children and adolescents. It ranks third among the causes of death among persons ages 15–24, although it may actually deserve a higher rank because many suicides are masked as accidents (Fredrick, 1985a). Basing his demographics upon data from the U.S. Census Bureau, and his suicide statistics upon data from the National Center for Health Statistics, Hendlin (1985) presents the following estimates of suicidal frequency in the United States. While there are some 27,000 completed suicides in the United States each year, some 20%, or 5,400, are 15–24 years of age. Shaffer and Fisher (1981) indicate that although the frequency of completed suicides is lower among children and early adolescents than in the older group, that number tends to be underrepresentative. In reviewing surveys of child psychiatric clinics in the United States and United Kingdom, they found that 7%–10% of all referrals were for the investigation or treatment of threatened or attempted suicide. They further indicate that suicidal children make up an even larger proportion of total referrals to child emergency or crisis clinics.

Michael Peck, director of the Los Angeles Suicide Prevention Center, differentiates six categories of youth suicide (Peck, 1984). These are useful in establishing both the age range and variety of motivations of suicidal children.

The Very Young (ages 10–14). Two characteristics are often noted in completed suicides among the very young. First, they tend to have experienced loss of a parent; second, they have a disproportionately high incidence of learning disabilities. Both factors tend to diminish a child's self-esteem.

The Loner. Frequently emerging from a family that defensively denies the child's dysphoria, thus creating the child's distrust for his or her own feelings, the loner is characterized by loneliness, isolation, lack of friends, and poor interpersonal communication. This type of suicidal youth represents a relatively higher potential for completed rather than failed suicide attempts.

Those Who Act Out Depression. Adolescents in this category use action as a coping mechanism in dealing with depressive feelings. They find actions that are rewarding in the short run, often illegal, dangerous, disruptive, harmful, or hostile behaviors such as drug/alcohol abuse, running away, petty crime, assaultive behavior, and serious violence. On the basis of clinical observations with 150 such patients in a psychiatric unit, Lustig and Zeitlin (1985) find two primary psychodynamic themes triggering the initial episode:

1. enormous fear of failure, creating a marked anxiety

2. reduced capacity to tolerate separation from people upon whom the youth is dependent

Failure means loss of identity and overwhelming anxiety, triggering antisocial behavior (Lustig & Zeitlin, 1985).

The Crisis Suicide. Representing less than 15% of all youth suicides, the crisis suicide presents no unusual background characteristics. The crisis, typically diagnosed as a reactive depression, follows sudden traumatic incidents and is characterized by dramatic behavioral change, hostility, and signs of confusion and disorganization.

Those Whose Suicidal Behavior Is a Form of Communication. This is a category characterized more by suicide attempts than by completed suicides. The behavior appears to be a "cry for help," usually does not follow prior attempts or accompany an "at-risk" profile, and sometimes results in an accidental death when a low-lethality plan goes wrong.

Discussions of background factors that are common among suicidal adolescents frequently reveal a broad range of factors, often cumulative in nature. Anderson (1981) points out that adolescents who have experienced significant object losses during childhood and who have grown up in unstable or hostile environments show greater suicidal risk. Teicher (1979) cites loss themes such as parental death, divorce and separation, stepparent problems, parental alcoholism, and frequent school changes as correlating significantly with suicide attempts.

Anderson's three-stage model of suicide provides some indication of why these background events are so significant. In the first stage, critical incidents and chronic problems together form a history that affects development, a history of vulnerability or risk. Adolescence creates a second stage of escalation of these problems. Behavioral changes that occur under the new stress of adolescence frequently serve to undermine social support and increase the experience of stress. The final stage involves a trigger situation, culminating in the suicide attempt. Thus a long-standing history of critical incidents provides the context within which a suicidal crisis develops.

RUNAWAYS

The National Center for Health conducted a study of the frequency of adolescent runaways in 1975 and reported that 10% of all youth between the ages of 12 and 17 run away one or more times (Justice & Duncan, 1976). This amounts to some 1,000,000 children under the age of 18, according to Walker (1975), who finds very little consensus in a literature survey regarding reasons to run away, except general agreement that disturbed family relations are involved.

Nilson (1981) compared runaway children to a control group in the areas of problem-solving abilities, coping skills, and background experiences. The control group consisted of nonrunaway referrals to counseling services, although the procedures used in selecting the sample were not clarified and so generalization is limited. Runaways did not differ significantly from controls with regard to coping or problem-solving skills, but ten times as many had family divorces, remarriages, and placements outside the home.

In a continuation of that study, Nilson explored the psychological profiles of 46 children: 28 runaways and 18 referrals from the same agency sources who approximated the runaways in terms of "need for supervision" but who had not run away. While family structure was similarly unstable and dysfunctional in both groups, runaways tended to have been abused or neglected more. Further, the runaway group tended to act out depressive features, showing higher rates of suicide ideation, gestures, and attempts.

Russell (1981), in his comparison of psychological profiles of runaways with delinquent referrals other than runaways from the same agencies, found more similarities than differences. Runaways differed from controls only in that there were a higher number from chaotic homes, and a greater percentage of runaways placed in the highest and lowest IQ ranges. Otherwise the groups were similar, showing the following exaggerated adolescent traits: self-centeredness, immature ego structures, interpersonal difficulties, and defective self-image. Half of the sample showed depression, while a third showed poor impulse control, regressive tendencies, emotional immaturity, and identity conflicts. Some 10% showed definite self-destructive signs.

On the basis of his research and review of the literature, Russell (1981) makes the following generalizations about runaways:

1. Running away is easier and a more socially acceptable form of protest in adolescence today.

2. There appear to be more neglectful, abusive, and conflictual homes today.

3. There are a greater number of incomplete or inadequately structured families unable to provide the emotional supports necessary to help accomplish the tasks of adolescence.

4. Most runaways manifest immature or incomplete development.

5. Running away can be seen as self-harming, or as a measure taken for protection against parental relationships or the adolescent's own expressions of rage (p. 72).

In terms of background and stressors, Russell's study bears further comment. Using his sample of 100 runaways drawn from a population of 2,000 juveniles court-referred for clinical evaluation, Russell reports the following background critical incidents:

1. divorce/separation, 49%

2. serious parental illness, 26%

3. severe parental alcoholism, 26%

4. death of a parent, 16%

SERIOUS SCHOOL ATTENDANCE PROBLEMS

Serious attendance problems continue to plague schools, despite the existence in many states of alternatives, such as the continuation school system in California, where each school district must provide a special setting for students at risk of dropping out.

In an early, comprehensive study of middle-class dropouts, Lichter, Rapien, Seibert, and Sklansky (1962) differentiated between what they called "psychological" and "reality" problems underlying serious nonattendance. Reality problems included lower IQ scores, economic need, and physical illness. Psychological problems, which accounted for the majority of dropout behavior, chiefly crystallized around issues of dependency and hostility, with parental characteristics projected upon teachers by the students (p. 40).

This projective dynamic may explain the reasons students frequently give for nonattendance, as summarized by Thorneburg (1975):

1. lack of interest

2. failing grades

3. relationship problems with teachers and peers

4. negative attitudes toward school

5. wanting to find a job

6. marriage and/or pregnancy

7. military enlistment

8. expulsion

The proposed relationship between underlying psychological needs and school nonattendance (as well as other maladaptive behaviors) is given support by the frequency of traumatic background factors among nonattenders. Harris (1980) provides the most thoroughly controlled documentation of this relationship, as previously discussed in this chapter. She showed significantly higher incidence of the following background events among nonattenders and at-risk-for-dropout subjects than among controls:

1. physical abuse

2. incest

3. sexual assault

4. death of a family member

5. divorce of parents

6. death of friend

7. frequency of school transfers

In addition, Harris found that dropout-prone students exhibited a higher total number of traumatic events, appeared to be more emotionally disturbed and in need of mental health services, and experienced higher levels of family stress within the past year than did controls. Finally, Harris found that these students exhibited more of the following maladaptive behaviors:

1. pregnancy

2. running away

3. delinquency

4. substance use/abuse

5. suicide attempts, and

6. self-mutilation

DRUG AND ALCOHOL ABUSE

The negative consequences of drug and alcohol abuse during adolescence are manifold. Accidents, violence (including assault, homicide, and suicide), overdose, physical and mental deterioration and disability, relational difficulties, and diminished work or school performance are all associated with drug and alcohol abuse during adolescence (Millman, Khuri, & Hammond, 1981). This litany includes the three leading causes of death among adolescents.

Drug and alcohol abuse differs from other maladaptive coping behaviors (such as running away, gambling, or risk taking) because, in addition to psychological dependence, it involves physiological dependence. Thus rehabilitation requires altering physiological as well as psychological cycles.

It is difficult to estimate abuse frequencies among adolescents, as the use of alcohol and drugs is such a pervasive part of the contemporary adolescent culture (and indeed of the general culture), and strict delineation of use from abuse is largely dependent upon the purpose of the person rendering the judgment. Millman et al. (1981) conceptualize substance use as having moved through an epidemic situation (precipitously increased usage) to the current endemic situation, in which use is an integral part of the rites of passage in America. Thus in 1977, Schukit, Morrissey, Lewis, and Buck estimated that 80% to 90% of adolescents are drinkers, and Abelson, Fishburn, and Cisin (1977) estimated that 15% of 14-year-olds and 31% of 18–21-year-olds use marijuana, based upon data gathered in a national survey on drug abuse sponsored by the U.S. Department of Health, Education and Welfare.

In many ways, alcohol and drug use makes sense to young people. In the process of moving from a position of relative dependence to one of relative independence, adolescents normally lack the sense of identity and personal competence to "be adult." In the short run, substance use provides peer acceptance, a sense of control, and a medicational effect, enhancing self-esteem and relieving anxiety and tension. Typical use begins with occasional experimentation in association with friends, usually beginning with alcohol and progressing to marijuana. Some adolescents move on to try depressants, stimulants, and psychedelics, culminating in opiates or cocaine. While most adolescents stop and stabilize at some point along this progression, some develop a poly-drug abuse pattern that varies according to the availability of the drugs, the situation, and the needs of the user (Millman et al., 1981).

A substantial determinant of early use patterns is peer group influence. In a review of the literature on the relationship between peer pressure and drug/alcohol abuse, Norem-Hebeison and Hedin (1981) conclude that adolescents derive progressively more support and information from peers, although the extent varies considerably.

Negligent or extreme parental styles often push adolescents into precocious identification with the peer group. This is borne out in the literature concerning background variables antecedent to problematic substance use. Robins, Davis, and Wish (1977) document increased incidence of parental divorce and separation in the backgrounds of substance-abusing adolescents. Similarly, Barnes (1979) found higher rates of family pathology among solvent abusers. Family alcoholism has also been found to be predictive of substance abuse.

Family pathology is one background factor predictive of substance abuse. Both victimization and loss during childhood are also predictive. Klagsbrun and Davis (1977), cited earlier, report a high correlation between parental loss and subsequent drug and alcohol abuse during adolescence. Similarly, Harris (1980), in her study of dropout-prone adolescents, showed substance abuse to be common among her sample and found high frequencies of both physical abuse and sexual assault in their backgrounds.

CONCLUSION

The research discussed here provides basic background information regarding childhood and adolescent crisis, and the connection between the two. The major forms of adolescent acting-out behaviors have been outlined in a manner designed to give professionals an overview of the central variables and dynamics of each. More important, these studies point to a relationship between childhood trauma and adolescent crisis that underscores the need for effective management of childhood crisis and illuminates essential dimensions of adolescent crisis.

Studies reviewed relating a range of antecedent experiences in childhood to subsequent specific maladaptive adolescent behaviors indicate a commonality of antecedents. Studies of adolescent alcohol and drug abuse, runaways, and serious school attendance problems show each to be positively correlated with incidents from the three thematic areas of critical incidents: family pathology, victimization, and loss. Only suicide was not correlated with all three; studies reviewed on suicide correlate that behavior with family pathology and loss, but not with victimization. It should be noted, however, that Briere, Runtz and Lightfoot (1978) have associated adult suicide with prior childhood sexual abuse.

This review of the literature relating to childhood critical incidents appears to support the contention that—in general—such incidents are related to maladaptive behaviors in adolescence. The one study that addressed this question directly established a connection (Harris, 1980). In addition, although each was limited in scope to specific childhood incidents or to specific behavioral consequences, the studies taken together add direct evidence to a general relationship and useful discussion of the dynamics of each aspect studied.

Appendix I of this volume reports original research supporting this general relationship and suggests approaches and management strategies for adults that are empirically associated with more healthy outcomes for traumatized children. The implications of this association will be discussed further in Chapter III.

Prior to that discussion, however, a major task remains. In order for professionals to determine appropriate steps to meet the challenge of childhood crises, it is essential that they know not only *that* an association exists between crisis and subsequent behavioral difficulties, but also *why* it exists and *how* it functions. We turn in the next chapter to this task and focus upon posttraumatic reactions in childhood.

CHAPTER II

CHILDREN'S REACTIONS TO TRAUMA

"This whole year has been just too crazy for me I guess. If things keep going on the way they are I am just going to bust out and seriously hurt somebody. I just want everybody to know one thing [that] I am _____ from 62nd St. East Coast Crips and I will always be a Crip no matter how old I get."

16-year-old who lost six cousins in unrelated deaths over a one-year period, three of which were gang-related.

OVERVIEW

When crisis occurs, school personnel need relevant, developmentally accurate information regarding children's reactions to trauma. This chapter provides detailed descriptions of children's reactions to crises, including typical aftereffects and developmental implications.

CHAPTER CONTENTS:

ACUTE SITUATIONAL REACTIONS TO CRISIS

POSTTRAUMATIC STRESS DISORDER
History—Contemporary Theories

PTSD IN CHILDREN
PTSD and Developmental Level—PTSD and Traumatized Groups—Typical Posttraumatic Behaviors—Developmental Implications— PTSD, Vietnam, and Implications for Traumatized Children

TRAUMA AND THE DEVELOPMENT OF MALADAPTIVE ADOLESCENT BEHAVIORS

CONCLUSION

PROFESSIONALS WHO WORK WITH CHILDREN, be they educators, therapists, social workers, or others, will encounter children whose lives have been changed by trauma. Effectiveness in dealing with such children during or after a crisis requires knowledge. In order to be aware of possible signs of trauma, professionals should first be able to recognize situations that are potentially traumatic. One doesn't need a Ph.D. to realize that most children will be traumatized by a parent's death, but there are other far less dramatic situations that are also potentially traumatic. For example:

> One woman in therapy for agoraphobia (fear of public places) had her most violent reactions when contemplating eating out in a restaurant. While the background factors were numerous and complex, one childhood event stood out in her mind. At about 11 years of age, following a move to the city and enrollment in a new, urban school, she was asked to give an oral report on her second day of school. Already having an upset stomach, she involuntarily vomited in front of the class. Not only had she never forgotten the incident, but whenever she went out in public she felt nauseated and frequently had to return home.

An experience that is only moderately difficult for one person may be unbearable and traumatic for another. Thus professionals cannot always gauge whether situations will be traumatic or not without observing the reactions of those involved.

Professionals in fields related to child care and child development need to become aware of the signs and symptoms of trauma. These symptoms may appear at times seemingly unrelated to crisis. While some children may have acute situational reactions to critical incidents that may manifest at the time of the incident or in the hours or days just following, a different set of symptoms may occur in the weeks, months, or years after the incident, and these delayed reactions may take many forms.

In this chapter the signs and symptoms of both acute situational stress and delayed stress reactions to critical incidents are outlined. The concept of Posttraumatic Stress Disorder is discussed as an explanatory construct, and the developmental implications of trauma are explored.

ACUTE SITUATIONAL REACTIONS TO CRISIS

Very little hard research has been (or can be) conducted on children's situational reactions to traumatic events. Much of what is recorded consists of inferences based upon secondhand reports of children's behavior during crises. Usually, rescue workers, police, and medical workers provide the most reliable information, and this section will draw heavily from such sources, as well as from the work of Eth and Pynoos, discussed later in the chapter. Their discussion of symptomatology is based upon observation of and interviews with children shortly after the children had witnessed a parent's death (Eth & Pynoos, 1985c).

Children's immediate responses to critical incidents can range from hysteria to shock. Often there is no apparent reaction— a visible response may set in only later. This is usually the result of denial: The child cannot make sense of the relevant sensory information and simply shuts it out. Sometimes the child lacks the conceptual maturity to comprehend what has happened. It is probably also often the case that adults observing children's reactions during such incidents are themselves caught up in the events, and therefore misread the children's subtle signs as lack of response.

In general, a child who is experiencing a traumatic reaction will show extremes of behavior, either underresponding or overresponding to the crisis situation. The signs and symptoms of acute stress in children can be grouped under the following classifications: cognitive, emotional, physical, and behavioral.

In order to obtain firsthand information regarding the specific reactions children go through following trauma, this author questioned 28 adolescents about their traumatic experiences. These adolescents were all at risk of dropping out of school, the majority were from middle-class families, and most were Anglo. Their experiences included rape, accidents, parental suicide attempts, divorce, death of parents or close friends, family problems, and abuse. And despite the fact that sexual abuse tends to be under-reported, some 36% of the females reported having been molested or raped.

The reactions listed below were each reported at least once by the group, and are representative of children's responses to a wide variety of critical incidents:

Signs and Symptoms of Situational Trauma

Cognitive	*Physical*
confusion	pounding heart
difficulties solving	nausea
problems	cramps
time distortions	sweating
problems in setting	other signs of shock
priorities	headaches
	muffled hearing
Emotional	*Behavioral*
irritability	slowness
fear	aimless wandering
anxiety	dejection
frustration	memory problems
anger	hysteria
	out-of-control behavior
	hyperactivity

This same group was asked which symptoms appeared weeks, months, and even years after the incident. They related the following signs of delayed response to the event:

Signs and Symptoms of Delayed Response to Trauma

Cognitive	*Physical*
confusion	fatigue
fear of going crazy	increased illness
preoccupation with the incident	
orientation toward the past	
denial of importance of the event	

Emotional	*Behavioral*
fear of reoccurrence	sleep problems
phobias	social withdrawal
oversensitivity	need to talk compulsively about the event
depression	
grief	relationship or family problems
guilt	
resentment	flashbacks
worry about physical health	avoidance of incident location
self-destructive behaviors	substance abuse

The delayed reactions listed here differ from immediate responses to trauma in some ways that might be expected. Yet the severity of the symptoms—sometimes years after the event—coupled with the fact that this group of young people had significant school attendance problems, higher-than-average rates of substance abuse, and other self-destructive behaviors, raises several interesting questions about posttraumatic stress reactions in childhood.

The most useful explanatory construct available for making sense of the relationship between traumas and later reactions is that of Posttraumatic Stress Disorder (PTSD). In the sections that follow, this construct will be explored, with particular emphasis upon the manner in which posttraumatic stress interacts with normal development and the evolution of symptomatology among children and adolescents.

POSTTRAUMATIC STRESS DISORDER

HISTORY

Over the years, practitioners have gradually formulated, applied, tested, and refined the concept of posttraumatic reactions. A quick review of the development of the concept may be useful, given that different aspects of the concept were the main focus in different eras. Freud's emphasis upon the stimulus barrier, for instance, is still of interest, even though current application of the concept does not employ Freudian terminology.

The concept of Posttraumatic Stress Disorder has a long and distinguished history, despite its fairly recent appearance as a diagnostic category in the American Psychiatric Association's (1980) *Diagnostic and Statistical Manual,* third edition (DSM-III). The disorder was described, at least symptomatically, in the writings of Shakespeare, Samuel Pepys, and Charles Dickens.

The concept of posttraumatic neurosis was introduced in the late nineteenth century and soon became a focus of controversy within English compensation laws following the expansion of railroads from freight to extensive passenger hauling (Trimble, 1981). In cases involving railroad passenger accidents, postaccident symptomatology was argued to be of psychological rather than physical origin, and this clearly had implications for settlements in court (Trimble, 1985). Subsequently, controversy over posttraumatic symptomatology spread to the battlefield, focusing upon whether "posttraumatic neurosis" was a legitimate clinical entity or simply a form of malingering.

Freud discussed traumatic experiences and their resulting sequelae in several writings, hypothesizing a protective shield, or stimulus barrier, that provides a threshold for the perception of stimulus (Freud, 1920, 1926). Once this stimulus barrier is breached, the pleasure principle no longer functions and the victim regresses to a more primitive form of functioning in order to master the stimulus. Helplessness is experienced, and obsessive repetition of the traumatic theme occurs. Defensive reactions may be utilized in order to avoid the painful repetitive stimulus (Freud, 1939). Elements of Freud's construct are found in contemporary theories of posttrauma reaction.

CONTEMPORARY THEORIES

The two major contemporary theories that explain the process of posttrauma reaction are based in cognitive psychology and learning theory, respectively. These theories are useful because they account for three common phenomena associated with posttrauma reactions: denial and numbing, reexperiencing, and depressive and phobic symptoms.

In the report of their work with Veterans Administration staff who treated Vietnam veterans, Horowitz and Solomon (1975) discuss two major dynamics that accounted for the delayed nature of the vets' stress responses. The first dynamic is what Freud had previously described as a "completion" tendency. In order to accommodate to a radically different situation that has changed as a result of a traumatic experience, memories, associated information, and implications are assimilated through a gradual process of integration. Primarily a cognitive process, this includes the intrusion of recurrent nightmares, daytime images and painful emotional reexperiences, unpleasant moods and emotional storms, and compulsive behavioral repetitions. This process may include secondary signs such as aggressive or self-destructive behavior, fear of loss of control over hostile or violent impulses characterized by apparent good functioning, and impaired social relationships. With veterans, such behavior often did not arise until years after return to a civilian life.

The second major dynamic is a "denial/numbing" tendency, serving as a defense against the intrusion of intolerable ideas and emotions. This tendency consists of denial, numbing, alienation, compartmentalization, and isolation of the traumatic experience from everyday life. Horowitz and Solomon believe that the denial/ numbing tendency interrupts the intrusion/repetition process, accounting for the delayed nature of Vietnam veterans' stress responses.

The intrusion/repetition process serves the healing function of integration and adaptation. The denial/numbing function appears to protect the individual from having to assimilate too much too soon. Horowitz and Solomon indicate that difficulties in integrating the Vietnam experience with the veterans' pre- and post-Vietnam lives leads to such psychological problems as low self-worth, shame, depersonalization, frustration and reactive rages, and various psychosocial disabilities.

Horowitz and Solomon's discussion builds upon Freud's, using essentially psychodynamic concepts. A learning model of posttrauma reaction is provided by Seligman and Garber (1980) in their discussion of learned helplessness. This is useful, as it presents a rationale for such symptoms as depression and phobias. Seligman and Garber describe traumatic situations as those in which adverse consequences follow a situation in which the victim perceives little or no control and little predictability. An externalized attribution of control is learned from the experience, forming a learned helplessness. On the basis of this, motivational deficits follow, and the victim ceases to initiate adaptive responses. Withdrawal, isolation, and depression are logical outcomes, as are anxieties and phobias resulting from the perception of the world as both threatening and unpredictable. Central to both Horowitz and Solomon's and Seligman and Garber's discussions is the nucleus of the posttrauma reaction: reexperience of the event, numbing of experience, and various forms of maladaptive behavioral change.

These theories make sense of such diverse phenomena, yet they appear to complicate understanding of the reaction with a wide variety of signs and symptoms. In order to provide a more cohesive description of the reaction, practitioners have sought to unify contemporary understanding into a single diagnostic formula in the latest edition of the American Psychiatric Association's *Diagnostic and Statistical Manual*, revised in 1987 (DSM-III-R). The reaction has been named Posttraumatic Stress Disorder, and the revised criteria for PTSD are now formalized as follows:

Diagnostic criteria for 309.89: Posttraumatic Stress Disorder

A. The person has experienced an event that is outside the range of usual human experience and that would be markedly distressing to almost anyone, e.g., serious threat to one's life or physical integrity; serious threat or harm to one's children, spouse, or other close relatives and friends; sudden destruction of one's home or community; or seeing another person who has recently been, or is being, seriously injured or killed as the result of an accident or physical violence.

B. The traumatic event is persistently reexperienced in at least one of the following ways:

1. recurrent and intrusive distressing recollections of the event (in young children, repetitive play in which themes or aspects of the trauma are expressed)

2. recurrent distressing dreams of the event

3. sudden acting or feeling as if the traumatic event were recurring (includes a sense of reliving the experience, illusions, hallucinations, and dissociative [flashback] episodes, even those that occur upon awakening or when intoxicated)

4. intense psychological distress at exposure to events that symbolize or resemble an aspect of the traumatic event, including anniversaries of the trauma

C. Persistent avoidance of stimuli associated with the trauma or numbing of general responsiveness (not present before the trauma), as indicated by at least three of the following:

1. efforts to avoid thoughts or feelings associated with the trauma

2. efforts to avoid activities or situations that arouse recollections of the trauma

3. inability to recall an important aspect of the trauma (psychogenic amnesia)

4. markedly diminished interest in significant activities (in young children, loss of recently acquired developmental skills such as toilet training or language skills)

5. feeling of detachment or estrangement from others

6. restricted range of affect, e.g., unable to have loving feelings

7. sense of a foreshortened future, e.g., does not expect to have a career, marriage, or children, or a long life

D. Persistent symptoms of increased arousal (not present before the trauma), as indicated by at least two of the following:

1. difficulty falling or staying asleep

2. irritability or outbursts of anger

3. difficulty concentrating

4. hypervigilance

5. exaggerated startle response

6. physiologic reactivity upon exposure to events that symbolize or resemble an aspect of the traumatic event (e.g., a woman who was raped in an elevator breaks out in a sweat when entering any elevator)

E. Duration of the disturbance (symptoms in B, C, and D) of at least one month.

Specify delayed onset if the onset of symptoms was at least six months after the trauma.

(American Psychiatric Association, 1987, pp. 250–251)

PTSD IN CHILDREN

The manner in which children are affected by PTSD is of great interest among educators and therapists because it directly affects the learning, behavior, and progress of children. While all but the most naïve accept that children are negatively affected by critical incidents in a lasting manner, *how* they are affected is less clear. Of equal importance to educators and others who work with children, however, is the need to know when to refer the child for extra services.

Until recently, little work had been done on articulating the specific manner in which PTSD is manifested in children. In general, there was a presumption that 1980 DSM-III criteria applied, but few verification studies had been done. Empirical studies regarding PTSD in children are beginning to surface through studies of specific situational stressors. Following the kidnaping of an entire busload of children in Chowchilla, California, Terr (1979) published the first of a series of studies describing the children's posttraumatic reactions. As early as 1976, Newman reported children's reactions to the disastrous Buffalo Creek flood. Pynoos and Eth (1984) describe children's reactions to witnessing parental homicide, and Earle (1979) studied the psychological effects upon children of mutilating surgery. Through these studies a clinical picture of PTSD in children is emerging.

In a brief review of contemporary thinking regarding childhood trauma, Benedek (1985) summarizes children's posttraumatic symptomatology as it applies to DSM-III PTSD criteria. Benedek cites in particular daydreams, fantasies, and nightmares (recurrent recollections), and behavioral changes linked to sudden visual and auditory stimuli that may remind children of the traumatic event. In addition, she notes emotional numbing in children, which she feels is in fact a defensive reaction:

> Particularly prominent in children are sleep disturbances, with inability to fall asleep, night terrors and nightmares. Traumatized children are described as regressing in the following ways: climbing in bed with their parents, sleeping in strange places, sucking their thumbs, and becoming enuretic. (Benedek, 1985, p. 8)

Benedek concludes that childhood symptomatology does indeed fit DSM-III criteria. As will be discussed below, the revised edition of the DSM-III (DSM-III-R; American Psychiatric Association, 1987) begins to address some of these issues.

Much remains to be done to clarify differences between childhood and adult Posttraumatic Stress Disorder. Diagnostic criteria and associated features must be refined further to provide a more precise clinical picture. As research and clinical knowledge sharpen, many children who have been diagnosed and treated as depressive, anxiety disordered, and adjustment disordered will be recognized to be suffering from PTSD. This change of diagnostic focus will bring about changes in treatment, as will be elaborated further in this chapter. Before treatment is addressed, however, the effect of developmental level must be considered, as well as the implications of PTSD in traumatized groups.

PTSD AND DEVELOPMENTAL LEVEL

Eth and Pynoos (1985c), working with a subject pool of trauma-tized children who had witnessed a parent's homicide and who were referred by various agencies for evaluation, describe develop-mental-level-specific posttraumatic symptomatology.

Based upon clinical interviews and treatment of 40 children who witnessed the homicide of a parent, Eth and Pynoos present a general phenomenology of posttraumatic reactions in childhood. They delineate specific developmental characteristics of pre-school, school-age, and adolescent groups and, on the basis of their literature review and observations, list common reactions to trau-ma occuring in children irrespective of their age. These general features include deleterious effects in the following areas:

1. Cognition
   recurrent and intrusive recollections
   decline in school performance
   learning problems
   misperception of duration and sequencing

2. Affect
   psychic numbing
   feelings of detachment
   constricted affect
   fear of repeated trauma
   anxiety
   feelings of guilt
   pessimistic expectations of the future
   intolerance of fear response

3. Interpersonal Relations

4. Behavior
   inhibited
   hypervigilant, avoidant, or phobic
   startle reactions
   reenactments; unknowing performance of similar acts
   repetitive, unsatisfying play involving traumatic themes
   counterphobic
   nightmares

5. Vegetative Function

6. Symptom Formation, including personality change

Posttraumatic features specific to preschool-age children include the following:

withdrawal, subdued and mute behavior
denial
participation in reenactments and unsatisfying plans involving traumatic themes
anxious attachment behaviors, including greater sep-aration or stranger anxiety, clinging to previously cherished objects, whining, crying, clinging, and tantrums
regression to previous levels of functioning
relatively brief grieving period
denial of permanence of change

Posttraumatic features specific to school-age children include:

lowering of intellectual functioning, school performance decline
inner plans of action (attempts at denial, compensation, reversal, or retribution through fantasy)
obsessive talking about incident
isolation of affect
constant anxious arousal
behavioral alterations
peer relational problems
more elaborate reenactments
psychosomatic complaints

Posttraumatic features specific to adolescents include the following:

premature closure of identity formation
acting-out behavior (including truancy, substance abuse, sexual activity)
self-criticism
fear of repetition of event in future (fate)

In general, Eth and Pynoos (1985c) point to the child's progress over developmental lines being accentuated, retarded, or fixated as current life circumstances are eroded by traumatic anxiety. Learning can be affected by constant reworking of traumatic memories, relationships can be altered by changes in emotional life, and major life decisions can be influenced by focus on the past (p. 50).

PTSD AND TRAUMATIZED GROUPS

In a fascinating recent paper, Terr (1985) discusses three subjects, each of which provides interesting information regarding children's reaction to trauma: the findings from the Chowchilla Group, which illustrate the differences between adults' and children's PTSD symptomatology; phenomena-specific group trauma; and five new findings concerning the experiences of children within traumatized groups. These discussions are summarized below.

The Chowchilla Group

In the late 1970s, Terr studied 25 youngsters who had been kidnaped as a group in Chowchilla, California. On the basis of field studies at the time and subsequent observations of children traumatized in separate, small group incidents, Terr draws the following conclusions regarding *PTSD symptoms unique to children:*

1. For the most part, children over 3–4 years of age do not become amnesic about their traumatic experiences. Unlike adults, who frequently deny external traumatic reality or repress memories, children tend to remember the experiences vividly. Children under 3–4 do tend to forget their experiences, due in part to repressions normal to the first few years of life and in part to nonverbal encoding of memories. Some children under 3–4 years will remember traumatic events, however.

2. For the most part, children do not experience the psychic numbing common to adults, with the exception of response to chronic stressors (such as parental abuse) as

opposed to acute stressors (such as an auto accident).

3. For the most part, children do not experience intrusive and disruptive visual flashbacks. Probably this is because children tend to daydream intentionally and have not engaged in significant denial of reality in the manner of adults.

4. Children's school performance usually does not decline in cases of acute trauma for as long a duration as adults' work performance is impaired.

5. Play and reenactment increase in frequency.

6. Time distortions are more frequent, including a foreshortened view of the future. (Terr, 1985, p. 51)

Phenomena-Specific Group Trauma

On the basis of clinical observations of Chowchilla children as a group and of four small groups of children who had, as groups, experienced traumatic events, Terr describes *posttraumatic group phenomena*. These phenomena do not automatically arise, nor is it possible to separate individual versus group determinates of a particular individual's manifesting a group symptom without extensive background investigation with that individual. These group phenomena are as follows:

1. symptom contagion affecting the group members and then their siblings, families, and associates (symptom contagion appears to be a large group phenomenon, as it was relatively insignificant among the small groups studied)

   a. posttraumatic play (trauma-theme specific)

   b. reenactment

   c. omens (irrational beliefs regarding the future based upon the event)

   d. foreshortened future (beliefs that a long-range future is not possible)

   e. fears and misperceptions

2. lack of group cohesiveness or breakdown of cohesiveness

3. failure of child victims to communicate verbally regarding the critical incident

Five New Findings

Terr's study of particular individuals within these different groups revealed several findings of interest regarding posttraumatic reactions among children:

1. *Ghosts:* Terr reports that children who have experienced sudden and shocking death sometimes see "ghosts," apparitions Terr attributes to posttraumatic misperception and hallucination.

2. *Time distortion:* While children prior to 12 years of age have not yet matured their time operations, observations of greater than expected time distortions are common among posttraumatic children. Overwhelming anxiety can distort time sense during critical incidents, leaving confusion and feelings of inadequacy later, particularly if the child must appear on the witness stand. Specific distortions include time compression and expansion. In addition, time distortions can make sequencing in memory difficult. A related phenomenon is future foreshortening, or the perception that future possibilities do not exist or have been precluded.

3. *Symbolization:* Parts of the traumatic experience may become symbolized by the child in forms more easily processed. What symbol is chosen and what part of the experience is chosen to be symbolized depend upon personal variables such as background experiences and issues, developmental level, and current situation.

4. *Condensation:* Separate ideas, symbols, or objects can be symbolized together. Symbols and condensations can be confusing and require astute observation to sort out.

5. *Preverbal memories:* Experiences of children under the age of 2 sometimes are encoded nonverbally; consequent-

ly, the children are unable to speak of a traumatic event. However, they can play out, reenact, or even show in concrete modes or fear responses what has happened to them. These memories appear to be preverbal and preconceptual.

Posttraumatic Stress Disorder is becoming accepted as a childhood clinical entity, as illustrated by recent studies. Arroyo and Eth (1985) diagnosed 10 of 30 referred children who had experienced war as suffering from PTSD. Fredrick (1985b), reviewing various literature sources, listed several psychiatric disturbances found among children. PTSD ranked seventh of ten in cases of disasters, first in cases of child molestation, and fourth in cases of physical abuse, although the sources of these figures are not clear.

In 1987 the diagnostic criteria for Posttraumatic Stress Disorder in DSM-III-R were adjusted to reflect the research that had been surfacing since 1980. These criteria include the following two unique to children:

B. (1) recurrent and intrusive distressing recollections of the event (in young children, repetitive play in which themes or aspects of the trauma are expressed)

C. (4) marked diminished interest in significant activities (in young children, loss of recently acquired developmental skills such as toilet training or language skills)

(American Psychiatric Association, 1987, p. 250)

In addition, further distinctive characteristics are discussed in a section on age-related features in the DSM-III-R (American Psychiatric Association, 1987, p. 249).

TYPICAL POSTTRAUMATIC BEHAVIORS

On the basis of the differing reports discussed so far, we see that children's reactions to crisis are varied, complex, and profound. However, patterns emerge that are cohesive, if not entirely predictable. Individual response patterns are limited by the child's state of development and personal history. The following summary description of typical posttraumatic behaviors may be useful to professionals observing children in their care. Note that each

progressive age may involve previous levels of functioning or malfunctioning in response to crisis.

The descriptions are keyed to general developmental stages.
They will prove useful for professionals in observing students in
the classroom setting for two reasons. First, observation of these
behaviors can alert staff members that a trauma may have occurred
in a particular child's life, recently or in the past. Appropriate steps
can be taken to corroborate this by questions or indirect inquiry.
Second, if the trauma has definitely occurred and remedial steps
have been taken, the knowledge that these behaviors are, in fact,
typical of posttraumatic children can give staff members the
needed perspective to deal effectively with the child in the school
setting. Knowing that certain abnormal behaviors are normal under
abnormal conditions is helpful and provides feedback for therapists
and parents.

It should also be noted that regression in functioning level is
a common response to anxiety. Thus posttraumatic behaviors typical of an earlier level of functioning may appear in an older child
or adult.

Preschool/Kindergarten Children

Posttraumatic behaviors that occur among preschool or kindergar-
ten children are likely to include the following:

Withdrawal. Children frequently react to trauma with a
generalized response of distrust. Perhaps because their cognitive
discriminatory processes are newly emergent, they cannot feel safe
from further harm. Also, children may try to assimilate their new
and very negative learning about the world. They may become un-
usually quiet or subdued and seemingly detached from others, and
may even become mute with adults or peers.

Denial. Children may deal with overwhelming experiences
and unbearable changes with denial. Denial may take many forms,
including denial of facts and memories of events, avoidance of certain themes or issues, and ignoring certain people or conditions.
This may be compounded by perceptual distortions and memory
gaps or embellishments that may occur with anyone, but particularly with younger children. This makes it difficult for adults to discern

when the child is denying, not remembering, or confusing facts.

Thematic Play. As children try to make sense out of traumatic experiences and the resulting life changes, the attempt must be cognitive, emotional, and relational. For children the best way to accomplish this is through play. Play is the medium they use normally to incorporate new ideas, realities, and feelings into their existing world, and it is not surprising that they use this medium in attempting to process the bigger issues they face. This includes frequent participation in reenactments or ritualistic play following a theme of either trauma itself or life upsets that are secondary to the trauma (such as family problems or physical changes). This can include playing horse, dolls, soldiers, or other such games either by themselves or with others. Children's art projects may also reflect traumatic themes and issues. Less obvious forms of play can include ritualistic interaction with parents or friends, fascination with certain themes in books or television, or solitary activity of a symbolic nature.

Anxious Attachment. Clinging, whining, not letting go of parents or of favorite objects, and tantrums are frequently signs of anxious attachment. Since attachment behavior occurs during this developmental stage with many nontraumatized children, changes in frequency and intensity are the best indications of such behavior influenced by trauma.

Specific Fears. Common specific fears include fear of new situations, strangers, males, confinement, violence, or certain objects. This may be noticeable in the classroom when a student becomes inappropriately emotional in an otherwise moderate situation, refuses to read a particular story, or won't talk about a certain subject. Sudden avoidance of the playground or reluctance to go home may surface. Problems with sleep may be fear reactions. Fear of going to sleep, nightmares, and frequent waking at night often develop because the cognitive dreamwork involves trauma-specific content or content having to do with loss brought about by changed circumstances.

Regression. Under severe stress, children attempt to master the situation by reverting to behavior patterns that were successful in earlier developmental stages. This represents a search for a comfort zone.

Younger School-Age Children

One or more of the above behaviors among preschool children are likely to resurface with school-age children in the face of post-traumatic adjustment stress. Posttraumatic behaviors likely to occur among school-age children include the following:

Performance Decline. A decline in performance may indicate a posttraumatic reaction among school-age children. School and intellectual performance as well as performance in sports, music lessons, and hobbies could all be affected. In the classroom a quiet child may drop from mostly As to mostly Ds in a short period of time with no explanation for the change. An athlete may begin missing practice or begin having a string of "off-days." The performance decline may be due to acting out, or it may be due to the child's preoccupation.

Compensatory Behavior. Behavior designed to compensate for the critical incident or its resulting loss, injury, or unwanted changes may be evident. Such behaviors may be attempts to deny or reverse the traumatic event, or to gain retribution through fantasy, play, or interaction. Compensatory themes in play may include killing the perpetrator, acting as if nothing had changed, or undoing the damage.

Obsessive Talking. Once the child feels free to talk about the incident, he or she may talk about it continually. Like a dam breaking, details about facts, interpretations, or reactions may spill out, unrestrained. The child may recount the incident again and again, and may repeat the theme in written work or in art. He or she may make resolutions, uncover feelings, and establish intimacy with others, but all this may be quickly undone when the processing is through. This necessary process of assimilating the event will be temporary.

Discrepancy in Mood. The child may exhibit feelings or moods inappropriate to the immediate situation or to the events he or she is describing. Sometimes this represents an attempt to avoid full realization, and at other times it is the result of the child's pre-occupation with past events. It may simply be a way of blocking communication regarding the event, possibly because the child is not ready to reopen wounds or because he or she does not yet trust the adult.

Behavior Changes or Problems. Children may exhibit changes in normal patterns of behavior. These changes do not always take the form of "problem" behaviors, but may nevertheless indicate underlying turmoil. They may get into trouble, or show sudden changes in interest, or regressive behavior. Often such changes result from children's attempts to relieve anxiety, gain needed attention, or sort through new, troubling information about the world and themselves.

More Elaborate Reenactments. School-age children's play tends to be more complex, abstract, and sophisticated than that of preschoolers; various personal themes and meanings permeate their activity. In their play, reenactments of traumatic events may become progressively more sophisticated, although often no more satisfactory than during early childhood. Developmental and incident-specific themes become scripts governing interaction and prompting tasks, decisions, and choices. As the child grows older, reenactments become less a function of indirect play and more a property of real-life transactions in the world.

Psychosomatic Complaints. If the excess stress caused by faltering attempts at posttrauma adjustment does not manifest itself in problematic behaviors, physical problems may occur. Some children show the effects of their difficult experience with physical complaints. Stomachaches, headaches, digestive upsets, and other physical disorders are often very real symptoms of psychological distress. Sometimes they are thinly disguised bids for extra time and attention. Such complaints are often indirect communications about other things.

Older School-Age Children/Adolescents

Behaviors specific to preschool or school-age children can resurface due to the tendency toward regression as a coping mechanism.

Posttraumatic behaviors likely to occur among older school-age children and adolescents include the following:

Acting-Out Behaviors. Perhaps because of a combination of peer influence and a need not to defer to parental support, adolescents often act out their distress in ways that are ultimately misguided and self-destructive. Typical patterns can include isolation, drug and alcohol abuse, sexual activity, violence, delinquency, running away, and suicidal expressions or attempts. While not every adolescent who engages in these behaviors has experienced trauma in the past, the majority have. The trauma may have been recent or long ago; even events distant in time may resurface with the increased developmental pressures of adolescence.

Low Self-Esteem and Self-Criticism. Adolescents are quick to blame themselves and to condemn their own reactions to crisis situations. They often have fanciful expectations regarding their control over situations; thus anything going wrong is a blow to their sense of power and independence.

"Too Old, Too Fast." Adolescents who are "too old, too fast" often are very reluctant to come to terms with their past experiences and resist interactions. Traumatized adolescents sometimes develop life-styles several years in advance of their age, particularly poor children, who must compete in the street with adults, and child prodigies, who constantly deal with adults. Such adolescents seem to expect a generally joyless existence; their life choices often confirm their expectations. They may take on unnecessary full-time jobs before high school graduation, or other heavy responsibilities such as a planned pregnancy or a decision to keep a baby when circumstances and attitudes clearly dictate otherwise.

Displaced Anger. Because teachers or other school personnel may be the safest people the adolescent confronts during the day, they may become the unwilling, undeserving recipients of anger that has no other place to go. This undeserved aggression certainly increases staff stress and makes school work unpleasant. Anger of this sort tends to be depersonalized and may seem ritualistic in nature.

Preoccupation with Self. Adolescents tend to see the world through their own colored glasses. They interpret an event on the basis of its impact on them first. Trauma and the resulting inner processing that must be done to sort through the meaning of the incident can intensify the adolescent's normal self-centeredness.

DEVELOPMENTAL IMPLICATIONS

A psychological trauma can interrupt the normal progress of development, causing more difficult resolution of current life issues and impeding growth. How this transpires is interesting in the sense that it provides a framework for understanding why a trauma can have its particular effect on a child's later life.

Human development consists of a gradual unfolding of personality wherein new learning and skills transform the individual from one state to another. Erickson (1968) describes this process as one of increasing differentiation, following a universal epigenic sequence. Individual development is shaped by cultural and familial influence interacting with genetically based aspects of personality. As social expectations change according to age and as hereditary traits manifest themselves, the individual is confronted with different demands. Each phase has certain inherent tasks that must be resolved to form the basis for further change. Erickson (1968) describes these steps as "crises."

> Each successive step then is a potential crisis because of a radical change in perspective. Crisis is used here in a developmental sense to connote not a threat of catastrophe but a turning point, a crucial period of increased vulnerability and heightened potential, and therefore the ontogenic source of generational strength and maladjustment (p. 96).

Erickson describes developmental crises as ontogenic sources of maladjustment as well as growth. Each successive stage of development, resulting from the external demands of environment interfacing with internal readiness for new levels of functioning, causes a specific vulnerability. A stage is a time when a given capacity or set of skills requisite to further development occurs—a turning point or crucial moment when the individual, as a result of both the acquisition of skills and capacities and the necessary cultural and biological pressure, must change. Unlike crisis in the sense of catastrophe, where the individual's resolution entails reestablishing a previous level of functioning, crisis here denotes an event or stage the resolution of which involves reaching previously unattained levels of functioning.

Development, then, is a process of transformation through stages characterized by specific demands, opportunities, and vulnerabilities. As Erickson suggests, adverse conditions may affect development in stage-specific ways. This disruption affects not only the stage during which the event occurred but also resolution of tasks in subsequent stages.

Two concepts are worth mentioning at this point, prior to exploring the effects of critical incidents upon developmental patterns: developmental anxiety and premature structuring.

In a discussion of the assessment of trait versus state anxiety, Saarni and Azara (1981) advance the concept of developmental anxiety. An extended state anxiety, developmental anxiety represents a reaction to the transition involved in the giving up of old forms of coping that worked at one level of development and the acquisition of new ones appropriate to a new level of development. The acquisition of new forms of coping can be a prolonged process of differentiation and experimentation and generates considerable anxiety.

Saarni and Azara (1981) interpret Erickson's "crisis" as a growth stage in which developmental anxiety "emerges and spurs the organism on afresh and with a new adaptiveness to synchronize forms of coping with the inherent conflicts of being alive" (p. 579). Thus developmental anxiety increases or decreases across the life span of the individual as that individual attempts resolution of each new set of demands raised by changes of biological and societal expectations.

Elkind (1981), in a book about the "hurried child" directed at a general audience and based upon an unclear methodology, discusses a concept that has some heuristic value. Premature structuring is a process by which character or personality formation of the child is accelerated due to the demands of the environment. This acts to constrict future personality development. Elkind cites child prodigies and children of slums as examples of children who must grow up too quickly, deal with grown-up demands and stressors too early, and develop certain aspects of their personalities at the expense of others. These children tend to become overspecialized and overdifferentiated in a manner that provides immediate survival value but closes off further learning and balanced growth. Particularly with prodigies, this premature structuring has serious consequences when the child reaches adolescence.

PTSD, VIETNAM, AND IMPLICATIONS FOR TRAUMATIZED CHILDREN

The notion of subsequent developmental implications following trauma was applied by Wilson (1978) in a major study of Vietnam veterans. The first part studied the personal attributes and perceptions of society of 56 veterans from the Cleveland area. As might be expected, Wilson found significant changes in ego-identity, ideology, and attitudes as a consequence of their involvement in the war. Adequately controlled by a sample of veterans who did not serve in Vietnam, this study utilized Erickson's developmental issues as a basis for determining developmental consequences of Vietnam combat.

Wilson found a wide range of symptomatology consistent with PTSD. He also determined that, as a group, combat veterans could be characterized as struggling with the developmental task of identity versus role confusion. Particularly difficult were adjustment to the existent social system of values and maintenance of a sense of self-sameness and continuity. Wilson characterized failure to develop a strong sense of coherency in a person as indicating a strong likelihood of suffering profound existential despair. The typical soldier in Vietnam was about 20 years old and had not had the opportunity to experience the sort of psychosocial moratorium Erickson considers essential for the exploration of ego boundaries and values as preparation for adult commitments. Combat critical incidents—indeed the social and moral tenor of the war itself— "constituted a series of social, moral, and psychosocial conflicts which were not easily assimilated into pre-existing cognitive structures or easily handled by emotional coping patterns" (Wilson, 1978, II, p. 1). Further, economic difficulties and social ambivalence toward the war deprived the veterans upon return of the sort of support needed for healing; thus they struggled against identity diffusion.

Compared to controls, Vietnam veterans' specific symptoms included the following:

1. difficulty in establishing a coherent and integrated sense of identity and successful intimate relationships

2. difficulty coping with interpersonal problems

3. more interpersonal conflict with significant others

4. greater drug use

5. lower career and educational aspirations

6. greater political and social alienation

7. psychic numbing

Wilson's results provide support for Erickson's (1968) contention that trauma during a particular psychosocial stage undermines the internal control mechanisms essential to development of the specific ego strength being formed during that period, or may exacerbate previously poorly developed ego strengths (such as mistrust, shame, or feelings of inferiority). Thus areas of potential weakness in ego development become at risk.

While the first volume of Wilson's study explored the manner in which combat experience negatively affected the successful resolution of the identity versus role confusion stage, the second focused upon the effects of the Vietnam combat experience upon subsequent developmental stages.

At the time Wilson wrote, the typical veteran was about 30 years old, faced with social demands for resolving the crisis of intimacy versus isolation. Wilson studied the love relationships and intimate personal friendships of the veterans, and found greater difficulty in relationships among veterans than among controls. He also found in veterans increased incidence of the following maladaptive means of dealing with interpersonal difficulties:

1. frequent and heavy use of drugs and alcohol

2. fits of anger

3. rage and hostility

4. emotional ambivalence toward loved ones

5. irresponsibility toward jobs and other commitments demanding propriety, reliability, and trustworthiness (p. 10)

Of particular note is Wilson's support of Erickson's notion of *distantiation*, or withdrawal from the sort of intimacy required to bring affection, sexual pleasure, love, and affiliation. Purposeful distantiation, a learned adaptive behavior in Vietnam, proved maladaptive at home, isolating the veteran from social support and impeding resolution of issues of identity.

Wilson's study supports Erickson's observations that each life stage is characterized by a particular psychosocial crisis and that each crisis bears the risk of specific types of ego-regressive attributes; sufficient stress and trauma during a specific stage will increase the risk of failing to master the critical issues and of developing the related ego-regressive attributes. Table 2 illustrates Erickson's regressive attributes of the various stages of child development as outlined by Wilson (1978, p. 28).

What was learned from Vietnam veterans can be transferred to the classroom, providing direction to professionals dealing with children who have been traumatized. Critical incidents require interventions geared toward the prevention of maladaptive behaviors in later development.

TRAUMA AND THE DEVELOPMENT OF MALADAPTIVE ADOLESCENT BEHAVIORS

Further research is needed to establish the correlation, if any, of the risk of specific types of maladaptive behaviors occurring as a result of childhood critical incidents (CCIs) taking place during specific developmental stages. PTSD, however, does provide an explanatory construct that is of value in understanding the high correlation of CCIs and maladaptive adolescent behaviors (MABs) in general. Traumas occurring during a specific developmental stage do create special vulnerabilities, by impeding successful resolution of growth issues during that stage, leaving the individual less able to resolve future issues successfully. Adolescence is a crucial stage,

Table 2: Developmental Ego-Regressive Attributes

Life Stage	Crisis	Ego-Regressive Attribute
infancy	trust versus mistrust	hopelessness, dependency, anxiety, withdrawal
play age	autonomy versus shame/doubt	overcontrol, impulsiveness, order, structure, predictability, helplessness
younger school age	initiative versus guilt	guilt, loss of rootedness, need for protectors, loss of purpose
older school age	industry versus inferiority	sense of futility, work paralysis, incompetence
adolescence	identity versus identity diffusion	self-consciousness, lack of commitment, prolonged moratorium

Source: Wilson (1978).

and the successful resolution of the issue of identity is particularly stressful and anxiety provoking when underlying issues (of mistrust, guilt, or feelings of inferiority) remain unresolved. The anxiety generated by outmoded coping mechanisms and new, seemingly insurmountable demands creates a propensity to adopt maladaptive coping strategies rather than no coping strategies at all.

CONCLUSION

The concept of PTSD provides a direction to use when approaching critical incidents and maladaptive behaviors as well. By recognizing the possible developmental outcomes of CCIs, clinicians, teachers, and other professionals can better plan comprehensive intervention approaches with traumatized children. Similarly, by recognizing the likelihood of prior CCIs in the lives of adolescents whose behavior is maladaptive and problematic, clinicians and student service professionals can plan interventions that can better address underlying causative and developmental factors.

Thus trauma produces psychological disequilibrium that is anxiety provoking. Attempts at coping with this anxiety affect the child's ability to tolerate the normal anxiety created by developmental transitions. The resulting combination can block successful developmental task mastery, and maladaptive attempts to cope with this anxiety can produce further complications. Such attempts can include typical adolescent acting-out behaviors such as premature structuring, extreme sensitivity to emotional issues, or self-defeating life choices.

With this understanding of the manner in which crises affect children's development, the way is cleared for an exploration of what professionals can do to minimize posttraumatic reactions and subsequent developmental difficulties.

CHAPTER III
WHAT THE SCHOOLS CAN DO

In order to see clearly the alternatives we face,
we must first distinguish education from
schooling, which means separating the
humanistic intent of the teacher from the impact
of the invariant structure of the school.

Ivan Illich, *The Alternative to Schooling*

OVERVIEW

*Despite the alarming increase in crises at school, school person-
nel are rarely trained in crisis management. They need guidelines
to follow when confronted with crisis situations. Therapists and
other mental health consultants would often like to help, but feel
unable to provide the programmatic approach teachers and administrators frequently want. This chapter provides such an approach.*

CHAPTER CONTENTS:

*WHAT TO EXPECT: POSTTRAUMATIC BEHAVIOR AT
SCHOOL*

GUIDELINES FOR INDIVIDUAL CONFERENCING

CLASSROOM DEBRIEFINGS

WHAT NOT TO DO

WHEN TO REFER

FOLLOW-THROUGH

CONCLUSION

SCHOOL PLAYS A UNIQUE ROLE in the lives of children, through its teachers, administrators, and other personnel. The child spends approximately six out of thirteen to fifteen waking hours in school. That is one-third to nearly one-half of the child's weekly life. Further, the school experience is a socializing and normalizing influence on children's lives. Events that happen to students individually affect their performance in class and affect the class as a whole. Events affecting the entire class have far-ranging effects in terms of classroom cohesiveness, school performance, learning, interpersonal relationships, behavior out of school, and the tendency toward behavioral problems later on.

This chapter explores what school personnel can do when students are exposed to traumatic events. Within one recent year, students watching television in their classrooms experienced the tragedy of the explosion of the space shuttle *Challenger*, students in the Midwest were held hostage by adults who placed a bomb in a classroom, and in Los Angeles a student put a gun to his head in an adult education classroom and pulled the trigger (fortunately, the gun did not discharge). More recently, in Illinois a young woman entered a second-grade classroom and began shooting, killing one child and wounding five others. These media-covered events are just examples of the thousands of critical incidents that affect the nation's classrooms annually. The manner in which school personnel respond to such events affects the traumatic impact they have on the children involved, both inside and outside the classroom.

Critical incidents are events that overwhelm an individual's capacity to cope. They are psychologically traumatic, causing emotional turmoil, cognitive problems, and behavioral changes. The effects of a critical incident can be lasting, depending upon the quality of the individual's experiences during or shortly after the incident. The degree and rate of recovery is determined in part by the extent to which the individual is surrounded by supportive, caring people who help him or her deal with the aftereffects of the experience.

The classroom is fertile ground for critical incidents. The group kidnaping at Chowchilla, the 49th Street School shooting in Los Angeles, and the shootings in Illinois are testimony to the possibility of large-scale, dramatic traumas. Yet far more frequent in the life of a class are such events as the victimization or death of a class member or the witnessing of shocking incidents by the group. Because classrooms are not insulated from the world, classroom events often occur in response to world events.

Following are responses to some questions frequently asked by school personnel about critical incidents:

How Often Do They Happen in a Classroom? Quite likely any given class will experience one and possibly several critical incidents in a year.

How Do They Affect a Class? An event that happens to one child affects other classmates vicariously. A class is an intimate group, and just as experiences of individual family members affect the rest of the family, one student's experiences will affect the rest of the class. Shared difficulties can bring classes together or pull them apart, affecting class climate, behavior, and performance.

What Is "Delayed Stress Response"? The immediate, situational response to a critical incident is called *acute stress response*. It is characterized by temporary problems in thinking, emotional overreactions (or underreactions), and behavioral changes. These responses are detailed in Chapter II. Sometimes the effects of the trauma do not surface for weeks, months, or years. This is called *delayed stress response*. Delayed stress response is generally thought to occur when the strategies used to cope with the critical incident prohibit the person from emotionally processing the event. Later, as the individual attempts to adapt to the changed circumstances, memories and feelings about the incident emerge, causing distress and further attempts at coping. Details about such responses to critical incidents may be found in Chapter II.

Why Must I Become Involved? School personnel must become involved in students' crises for two reasons. First, studies have shown that the way in which an adult responds to individual children and groups of children following a crisis can significantly affect the outcome of the experience. Through effective, caring intervention, negative delayed stress responses to trauma can be minimized. Second, the process of effectively intervening with individuals or groups is a tremendous group builder, creating a sense of cohesiveness in a class.

School staff members, particularly teachers, can provide several valuable services to their students that ultimately serve educa- tional goals. First, by becoming aware of the nature of incidents and posttraumatic behaviors, staff members are in a position to observe student reactions and respond correctly. Second, staff members can conference individually or work with an entire class for early intervention in a crisis situation. Third, they are in a position to provide effective coordination and follow-through with students, other staff, and parents. Finally, school personnel can interface in a knowledgeable manner with the school's mental health consultants or outside therapists to utilize these resources, when available, to their best effect. The following sections outline what an effective school team can do to assist and benefit from mental health specialists.

WHAT TO EXPECT:
POSTTRAUMATIC BEHAVIOR AT SCHOOL

The classroom setting is essentially naturalistic. This means that students are there in the normal course of events, not because they have been identified as "having a problem." Teachers and other school personnel observe children there day after day for hours at a time, so changes in the children's behavior are fairly obvious and changes over time are noticeable. When children's normal behavioral processes and development are altered by traumatic events, the school is one of the first places these changes are seen outside the home. Whether the original incident occurred in the classroom or elsewhere, classroom behavior is affected. Even if the child is under medical or psychological treatment for the trauma, school personnel will be in a situation to observe and deal with posttraumatic behavior. For purposes of identifying children who have been traumatized and for keeping perspective with children who staff already know have been traumatized, knowledge of post-trauma behavior is essential.

In dealing with children following a traumatic incident it is useful to know what to expect. Recovery behavior is different from everyday, regular behavior, in part because a great deal of inner work goes on in the assimilating process of the traumatic experience. Teachers need some sense of what is and is not "normal" during this unusual time.

In coping with the extreme stress of a critical incident, those going through it often suppress certain thoughts and feelings. This process allows the individual to do what must be done to maintain psychological and physical equilibrium. Traumatic experiences too threatening and disturbing to be assimilated at once gradually surface later to be fully integrated. This is a natural process of self-healing.

Trauma involves change. More than a simple emotional process, trauma forces the child to accommodate new, discrepant, and frequently threatening information about the world. The sudden realization of vulnerability, the loss of support or loved ones, or large-scale rejection requires difficult adjustments. As the child attempts to accommodate this new information cognitively, the thoughts and feelings associated with the incident begin to surface. The child reexperiences fear, anger, helplessness, and guilt. As the new changes in the child's life begin to be experienced, anxiety, fear, and depression may follow. The emotional reactions to this process can themselves make up a frightening, stressful, out-of-control experience.

Several general concepts regarding posttraumatic behavior in the classroom should be noted. These concepts provide an overall perspective regarding behavioral changes after trauma. Adults who work with traumatized children will benefit from this perspective because coping with posttraumatic behavior can be difficult, prolonged, and thankless. A realistic overview of the situation can do much to temper expectations and sustain willingness to persevere.

Normalcy. Emotional upset and faltering attempts to work out coping systems following a crisis are not indications of mental illness. Rather, they are very normal reactions to abnormal circumstances. To classify a person going through such reactions as crazy and assume that only psychologists are qualified to talk to him or her deprives that individual of much-needed support and healthy interaction. Staff members frequently feel that their training and scope of practice preclude them from being able to provide helpful contact with posttrauma children. This notion is mistaken; indeed, the opposite is the case. While psychotherapy is quite likely important, the *normalized* context of everyday life is essential to healing. Whether or not to refer a child to psychotherapy is another question that should be brought up with other staff members. See the section in this chapter titled "When to Refer."

Instability. Critical incidents alone, even the most severe, do not cause mental illness. Preexisting mental instability, however, may be reactivated by extreme stress. See the section "When to Refer" for further discussion regarding signs of more serious instability. Mental illness is an interesting concept within this culture, and great mystery surrounds its origin and treatment. Posttraumatic behavior may indeed be quite different from "normal" behavior, as the next section describes in detail. If posttraumatic changes are seen as attempts at adjustment, however, they will be less threatening. Staff must develop sufficient communication with the child to be able to talk about the behaviors within the context of school life.

Epicycles. Normal recovery can be a long process and probably will include times when it appears as though the child is getting worse, not better. Again, this is normal and is quite likely a part of the natural healing process. As the child becomes stronger, he or she is able to deal with more intense memories, thoughts, and feelings. Reactions to these intrusive memories and feelings can strain newly developed coping skills. Particularly difficult times can include anniversaries of the incident, similar situations, or events that preceded or coincided with the trauma event. These times can reawaken old hurts and cause difficulties. Often these appear to the child involved as reversals in progress. They may, however, represent real progress as the child deals with information thus far avoided.

Ages and Stages. Often years of relative calm go by without difficulty, and it appears that the crisis is really over. Then, suddenly, new problems arise. Normal developmental transitions create new realities, and these changes make a child's previously successful coping strategies obsolete. As short-term coping skills become outworn, new ones must develop. Until they do, painful memories become more intrusive and more difficult to manage. Often during these transitional times maladaptive behaviors develop as misguided attempts at coping. Adolescents, in particular, are likely to foster maladaptive attempts at adjustment.

Just as each person's experience of a particular incident is unique, responses to critical incidents are equally unique. Some patterns of behavioral change can be seen among individuals who have been traumatized, and the patterns of response to crisis particular to children show some common ties. The patterns manifested by an individual child, however, are limited by the child's own traits, personal background, and stage of development.

Classroom behaviors that can be expected following trauma were discussed at length in the previous chapter. Existence of these behaviors may indicate prior traumas, although they are not in themselves conclusive; more information is needed to corroborate these observations. The responsibility of educators is, however, to be aware of signals and to begin to try to account for children's posttrauma-type behavior. Gentle, general inquiry often leads to confirmation, as though the child was waiting for someone to ask. Other behaviors, put together, may form a pattern. The best context for such inquiry, as well as for providing support for the child, is the individual conference, discussed below.

GUIDELINES FOR INDIVIDUAL CONFERENCING

Sometimes the disclosures of critical incident experiences are direct and done in such a context that the class is not affected. When this is the case, teacher intervention can take place in individual conference without involving other students. Sometimes the individual disclosure is not direct, but the staff member observes suspicious behavior, writing, or art works. At this point nothing is known, but hypotheses can be formed. These hypotheses must be confirmed by corroborative information gathered through discussions with other staff, phone calls to the child's home, or direct conferences with the child.

Individual conferencing can occur in several situations. A student may have mentioned a critical incident in class discussion or in a writing assignment, prompting the teacher to inquire further. A student may ask to speak privately and then may take the teacher into his or her confidence. A student's performance or behavior may alert the teacher to a possible incident. Or perhaps the teacher has heard a disquieting rumor and wishes to provide the right context in case the student chooses to talk.

Approach styles differ among professionals. Some individuals can be very direct, while others are uncomfortable with this approach. Some may share their feelings openly, while others do not. Some styles of interaction are more helpful than others, however (see Appendix I). Styles that project judgmental attitudes, blaming, or general incompetence in dealing with the person or the content of disclosure tend to worsen the situation. Styles projecting warmth, caring, and a nonjudgmental attitude tend to be helpful. Beyond these basic differences, however, much latitude exists for personal style differences. In general, an authentic, honest approach is more conducive to trust than one that attempts to emulate the preconceived "right way."

The following strategies have proved helpful in dealing with distressed students in individual conferences:

1. Find a Comfortable, Private Place for the Conference. If the conference is individual, it must be private in order to engender trust. Audiences are inhibiting. A traumatized child or adolescent is usually embarrassed about his or her predicament. The social repercussions of gossip and hearsay are intimidating and will discourage disclosure. For this reason, providing a socially safe context is important. A word of caution is necessary, however. Educators must avoid placing themselves in compromising positions, particularly in the case of male teachers counseling female students. Stay visible to others.

2. Maintain Calm. In all probability, the student is experiencing uncertainty and self-doubt. Presenting a calm demeanor tells the student that what he or she is about to say will be accepted. On the other hand, the child must feel that the teacher is really present, attending, and nonjudgmental. This involves showing reactions. Professionals who are not normally as expressive as others should remember that in such situations they can express more without undermining the child's need to have an adult who can be trusted to handle information they consider revealing. In the study reported in Appendix I, adolescents reported that the worst thing their parents could do when facing the child's crisis was to fall apart and not be able to manage themselves or parent their children. While the proper balance between expression and calm is often hard to determine, a balanced demeanor is helpful.

3. Be Honest with Yourself. We all have days in which we are less effective than we can be. Further, we all have difficulty relating to certain issues or types of people. Recognizing such situations is essential. To attempt a conference with a troubled child in these circumstances would be a disservice to the child. Professionals need to keep in touch with their own feelings and their own reactions—to students, issues, and situations. If a teacher feels unable to handle the conference situation, he or she should ask someone else to take over, and should arrange a satisfactory transition, so that the child does not feel "passed off" or rejected.

4. Read Between the Lines. Often behavior belies speech. While a child is saying one thing, his or her body position, gestures, or facial expressions may be saying something else. Such incongruity may be significant. The professional should watch the student's behavior during a conference, and should be aware of subtle messages from which inferences for further exploration may be drawn. Finally, the professional should keep in mind how overt, nonverbal messages may be reflecting his or her own discomfort, judgments, or impatience.

5. Validate Feelings. Feelings are often barely, if at all, under control in times of crisis. They can be confused, contradictory, "inappropriate," or noticeably lacking. Feelings may be very strong under the surface, while the exterior may seem impassive and social. Feelings are neither right nor wrong. Whatever feelings the student is expressing during the conference, the professional should validate them as being present. Often many feelings clamor for expression; if the professional can help the student clarify them, it is very likely that they will change.

6. Listen Well. Listening is more than hearing. Listening implies attention, focus, and empathy. Children especially need to be listened to in a manner *they* recognize to be listening. Good listening involves several skills: gentle probes for clarification and elaboration, good eye contact, and the use of increasingly focused questions when appropriate (this is especially important when the professional suspects that harm has been done to a child). Professionals should trust their hunches, and check them out.

7. Show Belief. It is tempting to seek answers to questions about culpability. After all, if wrong has been done to the child, the conference provides an opportunity for a teacher to identify the wrongdoer and prevent further harm. It is also tempting to assume that the story is embellished, one-sided, or distorted, and that may indeed be the case. It is not the professional's role at this time to determine the accuracy of a child's report. To pursue the quest for truth or accuracy at this point is to violate the child's need to be heard. The professional's job is to listen and to facilitate expression. Not a judge, jury, or investigator, the professional serves as simply a helper or contact. He or she should show confidence, trust, and faith that the student is telling the truth as the student sees it. If the professional does believe that the child is being abused, however, he or she has a moral and probably a legal responsibility to report those suspicions to the proper authorities.

8. Dispel Fault. Children sometimes feel that a death, accident, or divorce is their fault, especially if they had thought angry or destructive thoughts prior to the event. In the need to stabilize their situation they may assume responsibility for events that are out of their control. Because they lack conceptual ability or experience, children may believe it when someone else tells them that they are at fault for a crisis. If the student has been victimized, the professional should make it clear that the incident was not the student's fault. The professional should be proactive about this, because victims tend to distrust and blame themselves.

9. Explore Fears. Individuals often are able to tell what happened to them, but unable to express assumptions they have made, questions they have, or fears they may hold about the incident. Helping a child to express these assumptions, questions, and fears may empower the child to deal with them. However, a cautionary note is in order here. Because perceptions under extreme stress are often inaccurate, even delusional, discussion of these perceptions may be an opportunity for the professional to provide a child with needed reality checks. However, it is important to contradict the child's perception as little as possible. This is not the time for the professional to act as judge and jury. The reality is that the child needs *support*. What he or she reports may be what is *true,* or it may be what he or she *fears* is true. The fears must be explored, facts that are clearly wrong and causing anguish must be clarified, and care must be taken to respect the child's need to express whatever needs expression at the time.

10. Provide Information. Providing the right information can be very helpful. If the professional knows something about the incident, normal reactions to that type of incident, or actions that could be taken, he or she should consider sharing it. He or she should be sure not to preach, however, and be sure that his or her own need to "do something" is not taking precedence over the child's needs. The most important consideration is whether or not the child is really ready for the information. The following questions can help the professional clarify whether children involved in a critical incident are ready for information:

do they need to vent feelings or to retell the incident more?
have they reached the point where the information meets a
    felt need?
do they have other investments in the situation that override
    the importance of the information?
do they want to hear?

11. Walk Through the Process. Many processes are predictable in any particular situation. Loss of a significant person will predictably involve the grief process. Disclosure of crime victimization will predictably involve police and legal procedures. When the time is right, a teacher's sharing what he or she knows about certain procedures can assist the student in predicting and planning for his or her near future. In addition, the professional's expectations for the present need to be stated.

12. Explore Resources. As soon as possible, the professional should explore with the student the resources available and what the student's support system provides. The professional should assist the student in deciding who is in his or her support group, and when and how to reach out for that support.

13. Find Friends. The professional may need to help the student to contact friends or family members, decide who at the school is available, and locate agencies or individuals in the community who could be of assistance. Professional and student should start with defining the needs and then move toward the solutions.

Teachers often shy away from dealing with troubled children, believing that they are not trained psychotherapists and are not being paid for this responsibility. The crucial distinction, however, is the difference between *doing therapy,* and managing a crisis in a manner that does not further traumatize the child through mishandling or neglect. Through individual conferencing in which the situation is shared, feelings are validated, and resources are explored, the negative impact of the trauma upon the overall educational experience is minimized. This is simply concerned crisis management in the service of learning.

CLASSROOM DEBRIEFINGS

Sometimes an entire class as a group is affected by a critical incident. A good example might be sharing the experience of watching the space shuttle explode on television. The death of a student, a natural disaster occurring during school hours, witnessing a violent crime as a group—these and many other situations present a need for group intervention. When the critical incident affects the entire group, it must be addressed with this group in mind.

Not only are crisis management courses not offered in teacher training, but basic principles of managing groups are similarly ignored. Students in teacher education take courses in educational philosophy, curriculum considerations, and discipline. However, this does not equip them to deal with groups of children who go through something out of the ordinary. A growing need exists for the development of principles and procedures that teachers and other educators can follow during times of crisis.

Procedures used by fire and rescue teams provide a useful and productive model for a group intervention. Jeffrey Mitchell of the Department of Emergency Health Services, University of Maryland, uses a group crisis intervention model with traumatized emergency teams. Critical Incident Stress Debriefing (CISD) holds promise as a structured intervention approach with groups of children, and the classroom debriefing format described here follows Mitchell's model. This model provides a definite procedure and system of rules for conducting such an activity, which is important when one is dealing with emotionally sensitive content. Students must feel secure before they can benefit.

Classroom debriefings are structured group discussions. Not intended or recommended to be psychotherapy, classroom debriefings allow the class as a group to sort out the events leading to the incident and to express reactions to the incident. Their purpose is to develop understanding and increased feelings of personal control. Debriefings are an attempt to salvage group cohesiveness from the disintegrating effects of a crisis.

Debriefings vary from group to group and from situation to situation, but they tend to follow five main phases:

1. Introductory Phase. The leader presents basic facts regarding the incident and lays down basic rules for participation. Rules for participation provide security for students. Talking about disturbing events is difficult; having a clear format spells out what the student can expect in terms of sequence of events in the group, confidentiality, what others will be talking about, and whether or not his or her feelings will be heard and respected. Much is at risk if the expression of feelings is allowed to have social backlash. The introductory phase is where the leader sets the tone for the entire session.

2. Fact Phase. Students explore and reach concurrence on the sequence of events and the role each played in the incident. Each student must be given several opportunities to describe each phase of the incident from his or her own perspective. By the time this is done thoroughly, the events will have been clarified for all, and everyone involved will have gained some realization that he or she was not alone in the experience. They will see that others were similarly affected, and a shared perspective of the incident will begin to emerge.

3. Feeling Phase. Feelings about the incident are explored in a supportive context. Each student is given the opportunity to share. Feelings are neither right nor wrong; they just are. Students have the right to express what they need to express and the responsibility to listen uncritically and supportively to what others are feeling. Again, it is important to stress that every student be given an opportunity—or several—to share his or her feelings, but that no student should *have* to share. Always announce the right to pass. To be coerced to share things that are uncomfortable is another victimization. It is important to explore what feelings were present during the incident and what feelings are present *now* concerning the incident.

4. Teaching Phase. Facts about posttraumatic response are shared with particular emphasis upon validation of individual experiences. The leader provides information to the students regarding normal reactions to the incident and anticipated reactions later. Any misconceptions regarding the incident or its effects can be cleared up. Finally, discussions and explorations of available resources can point out where to get help.

5. Closure Phase. A debriefing can be a significant event in the life of the group and can affirm group cohesiveness and the value of the group to the individuals within it. This can be summarized and final comments made by each student. It is often important to devise some actual plan of action the class can take to regain a feeling of at least partial control over fate. Invite further discussion at a later date on an individual or group basis.

The group's sense of security needs to be reestablished to a normal routine at the conclusion of the debriefing. The incident will have provided enough change for a while. Traumas are extreme disruptions, and the changes following traumas are further disruptions. Even class debriefings, designed to help students adjust, are themselves unsettling. A sense of continuity will be provided by a return to the normal events of the day. After the debriefing has run its course, the leader can do much for the students by letting them know clearly that the time has come to resume a normal routine.

The five phases of a class debriefing provide a structure that supports the individual and guides group process. Within this structure students can work toward a better understanding of the incident and its ramifications. The five stages are timed so as to maximize trust and sharing.

Following are some general suggestions for leading a group discussion after a crisis:

Leadership Style. The style of the leader can vary, but qualities of warmth, acceptance, and a nonthreatening nature combined with the ability to control the group process quietly are particularly helpful.

Opportunity for Sharing. Following a critical incident, students need a chance to talk about it. They do not, however, need to be coerced. The leader should make sure each student is asked questions at each step of the process, but should also set a rule that anyone can always say "pass" and not answer. Some clarification of this must be made in the introductory phase, during rule setting. This clarification is essential in lowering the anxiety level. A student can learn much, process much, and be helped a great deal simply by observing others and their reactions.

Ground Rules. Ground rules can vary group to group, but some standard and helpful ones are given below:

1. confidentiality ("What's said in here stays in here.")

2. no put-downs

3. no interrupting

4. speak only for yourself

Other rules can vary from group to group depending upon student needs, instructor preference, and the situation. Students may wish to specify particular rules with which they feel comfortable. The leader must be sure to check professional liability regarding the duty to report child abuse, dangerousness, and so on. These liabilities vary from state to state and can be a source of jeopardy for the unaware. The leader must make it clear to the group at the outset what the limits to his or her confidentiality are.

Format. One good way to handle the fact and feeling phases is for the leader to first go around the room asking individuals what they *saw* when they first became aware of the incident. Later, he or she should ask what individuals *heard,* and, finally, ask what they *felt.* This pattern establishes the principle of sharing while it moves from cognitive to affective material. The use of the term *felt* within the movement through the senses exploits the ambiguity of sensations versus feelings. This is a natural move and conducive to sharing and expression. Also, relating the material by "round robin" allows the reality of the experience to emerge and gives each individual increased opportunity and practice in participating before the content becomes uncontrollably emotional. In the event students jump at volunteering information, the leader can use his or her own judgment as to whether or not to allow open discussion. If open discussion is the decision, then care must be taken to ensure that each member has several opportunities to contribute. Further, the leader can choose to regulate the timing of the group in order to keep the discussion comfortable.

Needs. Students may need to talk about similar incidents, both current and past. This is all part of the sorting-out process and may occupy the majority of the time allotted. Often the present experience may be less serious than past incidents and a student may be talking about different events interchangeably or simultaneously without realizing it. The leader's clarification may be necessary to avoid confusion. Often one student will dominate the discussion and the leader will be forced to balance between the more acute needs of one or two individuals and the less acute needs of the majority (some of whom may also have acute needs, but may be quiet). The length of the session will be determined by the amount of obvious energy in the group. As long as it is focused and constructive, it should go on. If the session becomes unnecessarily uncomfortable for some member or digresses into unproductive chatter, it should be ended. Again, the tenor of the group will be fairly obvious and will provide the key to timing.

Reactions. Students' emotional reactions can vary widely. They can range from unaffected or amused to quite shaken. An "unaffected" reaction, however, may actually be numbness, and general amusement is often a defense against anxiety. Such students may need to be protected from others seeking to displace anger. In general, while reactions are bound to be strong, behavioral extremes are of concern. These are spelled out in this chapter in the section "When to Refer."

When It's Over. The leader should keep the discussion gently focused until it has run its course, and then get the classroom back to its normal routine. It is likely that students will still refer to the event and return to discussing it in the future. The object of debriefing after critical incidents is to open up discussion regarding the event. The teacher's job after debriefing is to be open to further discussion with students, whether it takes the form of class discussion, small group or individual interchange, written expression, or art work.

Assess. If students need further support (that is, if individuals are uncontrollable or seem to be in shock) the teacher should immediately refer them to the office or to whatever backup is available. This is discussed further in the section "When to Refer."

Teachers, auxiliary staff, and administrators need not be trained in psychotherapy in order to fill a therapeutic role effectively. The debriefing process modeled here is a management tool. The group being managed consists of students whose well-being coincides with the well-being of the group, and whose future academic learning depends in part upon their coming to understand an event that has befallen them. The purpose of classroom debriefings is not psychotherapy; rather, it is crisis management in service of education. The key actions involved include the establishment of ground rules, exploration of facts, sharing of feelings, and learning about future possibilities.

WHAT NOT TO DO

Much has been said so far about what to do with individuals and groups who have experienced traumatic situations. It would be irresponsible to indicate, however, that *any* interaction is preferable to no interaction at all. In the study reported in Appendix I, adolescents who had experienced trauma during childhood were questioned about how their parents had responded to them during and shortly after their critical incidents. The resulting styles of response were then matched with the children's subsequent adjustment. What emerged was a fairly clear picture of what does and does not work with children who have been subjected to traumatic experiences.

After a critical incident, the traumatized person is highly suggestible and emotionally vulnerable. Careless messages, heavy judgments, and bad advice can leave a lasting impression. Feelings of guilt, inadequacy, and social stigma can follow from well-meaning but hurtful "help" after a crisis. Such bad medicine can amount to retraumatization; the person is taught to hurt.

The study also indicates that there are two general types of interchange that are helpful to children in crisis. The discussions about individual conferencing and class debriefings have incorporated the helping behaviors common to those styles. The study further indicated that there were three styles of adult response that were *hurtful* to children following a crisis. These can be labeled as the withholding, incompetent, and reactive/escapist styles. Withholding parents tend to focus upon their own needs and deny the seriousness of the child's experience, shrugging off the child's feelings. Incompetent parents make false assurances, discourage discussion about the incident, and are themselves unable to cope or to continue fulfilling their normal role functions as parents. Reactive/escapist parents initially make false assumptions regarding the child's role in the incident and blame the child; later, these parents close communication regarding the incident. These three parenting styles during crisis were correlated with many problems for the child later, during the already difficult period of adolescence.

The study reported in Appendix I provides some indication of what *not* to do with a child or a group following a crisis. The following types of interaction should be *avoided* when talking to a student or class following a critical incident.

1. Falling Apart. It is essential that teachers and other professionals demonstrate empathy and understanding. It's all right for them to shed some tears in sympathy or express what they feel, but it is vital that they remain in emotional control. They must not fall apart or react with excessive emotion, because that sends a message that they can't be trusted with the information a student may give them. The student has enough to cope with; he or she does not need to be forced to take care of adults emotionally as well.

2. False promises. Professionals must not tell the individual or group things they are not really sure of or that are not true. If unsure of something, professionals should be careful to say so: "I'm not sure, but I will find out for you." They should not say, "Everything is going to be all right," unless they have some way of knowing that for sure.

3. Making Judgments. Facial expressions, body language, inferences, and questions can each communicate judgments. Even "Why did you take so long to come to me?" signals an implied judgment that may be more than a traumatized student can handle. The professional should focus on the person, not on what's "right." The child's needs must take precedence at this point.

4. Inquisition. The professional should not play detective, searching for information to identify the perpetrator. Pushing for information at this point comes across as using the child for other purposes. Such inquisition will only drive the student away or make things worse. Instead, the professional should assist the student in revealing what he or she feels necessary, and then work with that.

5. Role Defection. During crisis situations it is important for teachers to maintain control and not give up the leadership role. Students may complain about and resist classroom structure and discipline—the leadership of the teacher is sometimes seen as both a problem and a solution—yet students rely upon that structure for their sense of well-being. Discipline and leadership provide a secure base for the developing sense of self, a base against which to define one's individuality and personal values. The role filled by the teacher is important for any student; for the child in crisis, it is essential. Crisis threatens the existing structure of the world and the teacher, so it is important that the teacher in such a situation maintain a strong leadership and class structure, to provide a system of security.

6. Withdrawal. Professionals should not withdraw from children in crisis emotionally—enough stigma is attached to trauma as it is. If the trauma occurred at school, parents, relatives, and nonschool friends are likely to withdraw from traumatized children because they do not know what to do and feel incompetent. If the trauma occurred at home, school staff and students are likely to withdraw for the same reasons and also from the fear that they will make it worse. While the child in crisis does not need to be in the limelight, he or she does need to have supportive, normalizing, and affirming contact with others.

Students who have just been through traumatic situations do not need to be retraumatized by clumsy, heavy-handed intervention or by isolation and withdrawal. The maintenance of an ongoing classroom structure with caring, supportive, and listening school staff provides a healing context whether or not additional psychotherapy is needed or available. Important to the long-range management of student crisis is the follow-through that aware staff can provide. The following two sections discuss when referral is critical and ways in which school staff can provide helpful follow-through.

WHEN TO REFER

School personnel find themselves in a difficult predicament. While not trained as mental health specialists, they find themselves on the front lines when it comes to behavioral disturbances. When traumas occur at home, and sometimes they occur *because* of the home, school personnel are the first in the community to become aware of the children's behavioral changes. The section "What to Expect" outlined what school personnel can expect following a crisis. The behaviors outlined are "normal" following trauma. This section discusses behavior that is clearly extreme. The information will be useful to teachers and other professionals in determining when children should be referred for consultation with mental health specialists.

The question of when to refer is not a simple one, and no list of conditions can do more than provide general indicators. One difficulty is the question of degree of need. Anyone who has experienced trauma could probably benefit from professional consultation, if only to assess whether or not further intervention is needed. Specialists can provide support, perspective, assistance in family matters, and information about other resources. This would be a referral for purposes of *optimal* health and is optional. Many children who have experienced trauma can probably get along without treatment by a specialist. Some very serious signs, however, can indicate that mental health referral is important for the short- and long-range interests of a child. The teacher or administrator should always bring up concerns with guidance personnel and parents when questions arise, but this section addresses occasions when referral is critical.

The following guidelines are presented in an attempt to sharpen school staff perception of situations in which consideration of referral is essential. The main difference between normal and serious reactions to critical incidents is one of degree rather than kind. Serious reactions are simply normal reactions taken to an extreme; thus this section will differentiate between the normal reaction and its more serious counterpart. These signs will be grouped according to cognitive, emotional, and behavioral signs.

1. Cognitive Signs. A reaction may be said to be serious when

— slight disorientation has become the inability to tell one's name, the date, or relate what has happened over the past 24 hours.

— too much concern over little things has become exclusive preoccupation with one idea.

— denial of the severity of the problem has become wholesale denial that a problem exists.

— visual or auditory flashbacks have become out-of-control hallucinations.

— self-doubt has become a feeling of unreality, disconnectedness, fear of "losing my mind."

— difficulty in planning practical things has become the inability to carry out basic life functions.

— light confusion has become bizarre, irrational beliefs, and these form the basis for action.

2. Emotional Signs. A reaction may be said to be serious when

— crying has become uncontrolled hysteria.

— anger or self-blame has become fear or threats of harm to self or others.

— blunted emotional response or numbing has become complete withdrawal, with no emotional response.

— appropriate expression of despair or depression has become self-destructive.

3. Behavioral Signs. A reaction may be said to be serious when

— restlessness or excitement has become unfocused agitation.

— excessive talking or nervous laughter has become uncontrolled.

— frequent retelling of the incident has become continual or ritualistic.

— pacing, hand-wringing, or fist-clenching has become ritualistic or uncontrolled.

— disheveled appearance has, over time, become an inability to care for oneself.

— irritability has become destructive.

Referral is sometimes made for reasons of optimal adjustment. Sometimes, in cases such as those described above, in which a child's behavior indicates serious disturbance, the care of specialists is required to prevent even worse decline. While teachers are usually the ones who raise the questions, referrals themselves are usually made by district psychologists or administrators. Often the teacher is then left with no indication of what might happen to the child. Chapter IV, "What Therapists Can Do," is designed to shed light upon the black box of therapeutic process, and school personnel are urged to read that chapter to obtain greater understanding of what happens in therapy. In addition, the next section addresses the issues involved in school follow-through.

FOLLOW-THROUGH

The process of classroom management of crisis does not end with a formal conference or debriefing or even with referral of some students for mental health services. Staff follow-through is important in four particular areas: in the classroom itself, with other staff members, with auxiliary personnel such as outside therapists, and with the child's family.

In the classroom, the fact that the trauma occurred is inescapable. After conferences and debriefing, the cognitive, emotional, and social processing of the event continues. If the event occurred outside of class to one student, it is quite likely that little explicit mention of the incident will be made. Instead, the child may deal with it indirectly through art, writing, thematic play, or choices of reading material. The child may talk to the teacher or to a circle of friends about it. The teacher, school psychologist, or other staff member can encourage or even facilitate this attempt at dealing with the changes the trauma has brought about.

If the event occurred to the group as a whole, it is likely to occur as an object of discussion as well as in the indirect ways mentioned above. This is an opportunity for group building of the class, and the honesty and straightforward nature of the debriefing can extend to other classroom contexts. The processes of assimilation and accommodation should be encouraged, and the teacher can raise the issue through various class activities. Eventually, if given sufficient attention over time, the traumatic event will become old news without being repressed by group taboo. Some groups may resist rehashing the event. Since there is a tendency to avoid confronting painful material, initial reluctance may occur.

Follow-through with staff members varies in form depending

upon the interpersonal makeup of the staff, its normal mode of communication, the roles staff members have played in the crisis, and the types of specialists available.

If the crisis occurred outside of the school and is limited to one student, follow-through may be needed only with the teacher, the administrator, and any other support personnel who have been involved. This may consist of informed periodic status reports, but it may also include consultation for brainstorming and problem solving to ensure that educational services to the child are well maintained through the aftermath of the crisis.

If the crisis occurred in the class, more personnel are likely to be involved, particularly district staff. The event will be more organizationally visible and perhaps more visible to the community. There may be more pressure upon the organization to portray a proactive stance in dealing with the crisis. Administrators may exhibit more involvement with activity planning and may ask the teacher for more frequent and formal status reports and articulated action plans. Other staff members will be more interested, and periodic updates will be expected. The stress on the teaching staff and students will be more intense.

Finally, if the event occurred to several classes at once, the visibility will be even greater. Besides the need for greater resources and thoughts regarding methods of meeting the diversity of personal needs, new levels of organizational needs will emerge. Resources will have to be allocated in an effective manner. Information will have to be organized and communicated consistently. School activities will need to be coordinated appropriately. There is likely to be increased community awareness, and this may entail media coverage. Media coverage will affect staff members, increasing staff stress and contributing to a general sense of emergency. Uninvolved students will pick up on the excitement and need to be apprised of as much information as is appropriate. In order to avoid the effects of rumormongering, a consistent, regular updating of information is essential. In addition, all students will need time to talk about not only the crisis and its residual effects but also the subsequent and current development.

Follow-up can also be conducted with any mental health professionals who are involved. While updating is a major part of such an effort, it has more to do with enhancing concurrent treatment. Therapists become involved in two major capacities. First, they may be consulting with school personnel or even working with students or whole classes themselves. In this capacity, their primary source of valid information consists of the observations of the classroom teacher. The information they will seek will include the general class mood, specific incidents that are indicative of underlying issues, the extent to which children are communicative about these issues, problems that have arisen, and particular individuals who seem to be having a rougher-than-average time. Contact between the consultant and school personnel regarding progress and the effects of specific activities can increase the effectiveness of the consultant.

The other major capacity in which therapists become involved is in treating individual students apart from the school. It is often the case that school personnel make referrals to therapists, and then assume that the problem is gone. This severance of services limits the effectiveness of each. Educators need information regarding the progress and needs of their students who are receiving mental health services in order to manage wisely for educational gain. Therapists can similarly gain from teacher feedback regarding a child's classroom behavior. The school exists in "real time" for children. It is a natural setting, while the clinical office is not. Therapists deal mainly with inferences drawn from secondhand information and self-report. Teachers can provide the therapist extensive observation of the child's individual and social behavior in his or her normal world. However, to most teachers, therapy is a "black box." The lack of experience shared by teachers and therapists limits their communication. With the perspectives provided in this book, teachers and therapists may begin to utilize their knowledge of each other's function in order to ask the right questions and give the right answers.

Parents represent the final area for follow-through. As mentioned earlier, families often present significant resistance to communication about their children's traumatic experiences. No one raises a child to be hurt. Most parents are appalled at the idea of their children being hurt, even in some cases where they themselves are the ones inflicting the pain. The natural first reaction to bad news is denial, and parental resistance to dealing openly with children's hurt is a form of denial. Second, a child's hurt may cause unpleasant memories of the parent's own past hurts, and this may spark a desire to avoid thinking about it. Another source of resistance lies in the fact that trauma often uncovers weaknesses in the fabric of the family relationship. If that is the case, a child's needs may go unmet because to deal with them might cost the whole family. Another source of resistance is feelings of shame because the event has occurred. Finally, many forms of resistance are grounded in the family's general resistance to being intruded upon by yet another bureaucratic institution.

Whatever the source of resistance, it makes the task of the school more difficult. However, the degree of resistance is usually a good indication of how much the child needs the school to make the contact and to open up communication. The specific form of parent contact need not differ from other school-home communication, except that it needs to be personal contact and not form letters. Further, if the trauma involved the group, continued information about what activities are being done in class to deal with the incident helps keep parents involved. Likewise, calls or questionnaires with personal notes requesting information about behavioral changes noticed at school not only provide helpful information, but also keep the door open for future contact.

CONCLUSION

Crisis can occur in or out of school, but in either case the school is involved. The child's behavior is affected and the class climate and productivity will undergo change.

Teachers and administrators can assist the child and the class by providing a context within which the child is safe. This entails doing some things and avoiding others, as was discussed. The gravity of the crisis should not create a fear of contact with involved students and professional therapists. Much can be done by people without specialized training, and, in fact, much should be done by school personnel. While certain types of interaction need to be avoided, specific positive steps can be taken in the proactive management of the crisis situation. These steps have been outlined in the sections on individual conferencing, class debriefing, and follow-through. Awareness of specific signs that indicate when referral is appropriate can ensure that those referrals are made in a timely manner; this awareness can also assist school staff in interfacing with district psychologists and outside mental health consultants for the student's benefit. Finally, such a proactive posture helps school personnel deal with the children's families, who are likely to be in very real pain.

CHAPTER IV

WHAT THERAPISTS CAN DO

We had all been believers, believers in ourselves
and hence the future. But events have driven a
barrier between the past and the present, and we
are now all refugees in our own country.

> Peter Shrag, *Out of Place in America*

Extreme remedies are very appropriate for
extreme diseases.

> Hippocrates, *Aphorisms*

Who, doomed to go in company with Pain,
And Fear; and Bloodshed, miserable train!
Turns his necessity to glorious gain . . .

> William Wordsworth,
> "Character of the Happy Warrior"

OVERVIEW

*For most school personnel, what goes on in psychotherapy remains
a mystery. Without a basic understanding of the direction and process of therapy, educators often feel unable to work with therapists.
In addition, many therapists who do not regularly work with traumatized children do not feel comfortable in dealing with either the
children or their families. This chapter distinguishes between
crisis intervention and psychological treatment, defines the central
task of therapy, and describes methods of child and adolescent
treatment. In addition, it specifies information from natural settings that therapists can use, opening the door to the therapeutic
process for nonclinicians.*

TRAUMATIZED CHILDREN are seen in a clinical setting for a variety of reasons. Central to their successful treatment is the management of their posttraumatic reaction, whether this occurs as the focus or as a component of treatment. Understanding the reaction is the first necessary part of treatment. Then, however, the work of reexperiencing, releasing, and integrating the experience must begin. The various treatment modalities employed with traumatized children, such as art and play therapy, aim at reexperience/ release/integration. This chapter explores this process, starting with general considerations regarding course of treatment.

The purpose of such a discussion is twofold. First, clinicians typically have broad-based training in doing therapy and have developed skills in particular methods. In addition, detailed literature and training abounds in specific treatment approaches. Less attention is paid, however, to articulating a clear statement of clinical directions and overall treatment progress with traumatized children. This chapter seeks to provide such a statement irrespective of treatment approach.

Second, nonclinicians such as educators, clergy, or others working with children are often faced with traumatized children. They need more than simply a few signs when contemplating referring a child or family for therapy. A basic understanding of what goes on—or should go on—in therapy will provide a better basis for decisions regarding referral. A clear statement of clinical directions will help as well.

Therapists deal with posttraumatic children in three contexts:

1. just after the trauma, upon referral

2. months later, for trauma-specific symptoms such as nightmares, phobias, or adjustment problems

3. much later, during developmental transition periods, when coping patterns have become problematic

Most of the cases of delayed reaction to traumas manifest indirect symptoms. The real value of a firm understanding of posttraumatic stress is heuristic. For those cases where client symptomatology *could be* indicative of prior trauma, inquiry into background experiences is *likely* to turn up such experiences. This, in turn, may indicate that dealing with the trauma may be an essential part of treatment.

Posttraumatic Stress Disorder provides a direction for investigation when approaching critical incidents and maladaptive behaviors as well. By recognizing the possible developmental outcomes of trauma, clinicians and other adults can better plan comprehensive intervention approaches with traumatized children. Similarly, by recognizing the likelihood of prior trauma in the lives of adolescents whose behavior is maladaptive and problematic, clinicians and others can plan interventions that better address underlying causative factors.

THE THERAPEUTIC TASK

When approaching these questions, an understanding of the normative process of trauma adjustment is important. Horowitz (1976) describes an "ideal course" for the adjustment to a critical incident: Recovery is maximized if the person

1. perceives the event correctly

2. translates the perceptions into a clear meaning

3. relates the meaning to an enduring attitude

4. decides on an appropriate action, and

5. revises memories, attitudes, and belief systems to fit a new developmental line made necessary by the experience (cited in Donaldson & Gardner, 1985)

This model was developed by Horowitz from his work with Vietnam veterans. As such, it is framed for adults within a specific developmental context (for more on this subject, see the discussion of Wilson's work in Chapter II). While the developmental context differs for children, the model applies equally to them and provides a concise statement of treatment goals.

Donaldson and Gardner (1985) further expand upon Horowitz's model to generate the following treatment implications:

1. After a traumatic event, the afflicted person is less bothered in later life if he or she undergoes an ideal psychological processing (Horowitz's "ideal course")

2. This ideal course is interfered with by overly powerful memories persisting in "active memory storage" when "processing" does not occur

3. Therapeutic information breaks the cyclical alternating of denial and numbing and intrusive repetitious thoughts by providing a safe environment in which one can experience the emotional response without automatic denial and numbing of the emotions

4. Simple conscious recollections, emotional catharses, or reviews of one's thoughts and beliefs are not enough by themselves but must proceed simultaneously and repeatedly for the best working-through process (p. 368)

The posttraumatic reaction does not occur in a social or developmental vacuum. Treatment of trauma-specific symptoms usually takes place along with treatment of other problems secondary to the trauma, such as behavior problems, school difficulties, and family interaction. Attempts by the individual at coping with the trauma over time have a detrimental effect upon all aspects of development. The clinician is rarely presented with posttrauma cases that are simple, (simple, that is, in the sense that there is an absence of complicating factors).

TREATMENT CONSIDERATIONS WITH TRAUMATIZED CHILDREN

Clinicians working with traumatized children should adapt the general model of trauma processing to children's developmental levels and needs. This includes a sensitivity to the differences between various age groups and the exigencies of particular situations. The need for delicate assessment of the child's needs, strengths, and situation is apparent. This section will consider several factors to be taken into account by therapists assessing cases of trauma. Following a discussion of child-specific symptoms, various approaches to clinical assessment will be considered. At this point, some approaches to treatment can be described.

Children who have experienced critical incidents are at risk for subsequent maladaptive behavior as well as for various situational symptoms. Terr (1981) lists some of these child-specific symptoms:

1. fear of death, separation, and further trauma

2. misidentification of perpetrators and/or hallucinations of perpetrators

3. no disavowal or traumatic amnesia

4. absent vegetative or nervous effects

These are "child-specific" in the sense that they frequently occur with children and manifest in a manner consistent with developmental level, although they do occur normally with adults due to the regressive nature of response to trauma.

Interestingly, Terr (1985) and Nir (1985) differ as to the presence of intrusive imagery. As mentioned in Chapter II, Terr (1985) has reported that children do not experience intrusive imagery or flashbacks. Nir (1985), reporting upon observations of childhood postcancer patients, indicates that intrusive recollections, repetitive dreams, and nightmares definitely occur. Perhaps Terr does not consider memories or dreams intrusive imagery, or perhaps Nir does not refer to flashbacks, but there seems to be a discrepancy in their reports. One possible explanation for this might be the differences in type of trauma experienced by the subjects studied by these two authors. Terr studied victims of high-intensity, single-incident trauma, while Nir observed cancer victims—children exposed to a long-duration, chronic stressor. It may be that chronic stressors result in intrusive imagery in ways that single-incident stressors do not. This issue warrants empirical resolution, as it is of some importance whether intrusive images are a function of developmental level or of type of incident.

It must be stated again that the clinical understanding of posttraumatic reactions with children is barely past its infancy. Much of the major empirical research regarding child-specific posttraumatic symptomatology is fairly recent. Controversy exists regarding various issues; the intrusive imagery issue is one. Another is the extent to which natural disasters are traumatic. As the clinical debates mount, it can be expected that research directions and methodology will sharpen and that more light will be shed upon the clinical picture. As research, funding, and treatment innovations intensify, practitioners will have clearer guidelines for making decisions regarding appropriateness of treatment modalities and indications for referral.

ASSESSMENT

The fact that there exist no universally accepted standards for assessment protocol is a reflection of the relative infancy of the discipline. Clinicians frequently have difficulty determining just what behaviors are symptomatic of trauma and indicative of specific treatment needs and what behaviors are part of other clinical pictures. In discussing treatment considerations, then, adequate assessment is paramount. Scurfield (1985) outlines four elements in a comprehensive assessment of posttraumatic stress reaction. Designed for adults, in principle they provide a framework for child assessment as well:

1. **Pretrauma History.** Parental and peer relationships, behavior patterns at home and school, preexisting behavioral disorders, social context, and stressors should be explored, with par-

ticular focus upon pre- and posttrauma differences.

2. Immediate Pretrauma Psychosocial Context. Age and developmental level, as well as particular familial, social, or developmental issues, bear heavily on the meaning of the event, means of coping, and resources available.

3. Traumatic Events and Immediate (Emergency) Coping Attempts. Objective factors such as the frequency, intensity, and nature of the event can each have different ramifications. The role (active or passive) played by the individual and the meaning of the event to the individual must be assessed, as well as immediate reactions to the event.

4. Posttraumatic Psychosocial Context and Reactions. The effects of the environment (as supportive or problematic) must be explored in terms of specific resources and liabilities. Posttraumatic symptomatology must be considered.

Eth and Pynoos (1985a), based upon their clinical experience and literature review, list a range of features manifested by children who have undergone acute posttraumatic stress:

1. exhibition of paralysis and immobilization, ranging from numbness to emotional storms; disorganized feelings, thoughts, and behavior; physical symptoms reflecting autonomic dysfunction

2. frozen, pale, or submissive appearance, or frenzied and panicked behavior

3. aimless, frenzied overactivity, sometimes culminating in tantrums or rage, or a shocklike, stunned reaction, presenting various degrees of unresponsiveness, inactivity, or torpor (p. 39)

4. predifferentiation (disorganization and primitivization of thoughts), deverbalization, and resomatization of affect (p. 46)

To assess such features adequately and make sense of them within the context of the child's experiences, Eth and Pynoos (1985b) utilize the following assessment protocol. Prior to the interview proper, information is gathered from the referral source. Then the child is asked to draw a picture, of his or her choice. Sometimes the content of the trauma emerges directly; frequently, coping and defense maneuvers to minimize anxiety are evident. Second, the interviewer explores the child's perception of the traumatic event, with particular focus upon the child's perceptual and affective experiences, issues of accountability and impulse control, and past traumas. Drawing or reenactments of the event, fantasies of revenge, or other issues are sometimes utilized. During the third and closing phase, present and future life concerns are reviewed, mourning is supported, and the interview is reviewed. Follow-up contacts are made available.

It should be noted that the referral source is only one means of obtaining background information. Parents, siblings, grandparents, and friends can provide detailed information regarding past history, individual characteristics, interests and issues, and recent changes. They can also provide—directly and indirectly—perspective on the family context. Other background resources can include school personnel and records, church contacts, or social agencies.

Fredrick (1985b) points out five nonverbal signs of posttraumatic stress that are of special note in assessment, particularly among younger children:

1. sleep disturbances continuing more than several days, wherein actual dreams of the trauma may or may not appear

2. separation anxiety or clinging behavior, such as a reluctance to return to school

3. phobias about distressing stimuli (e.g., school building, TV scenes, or persons) that remind the victim of the traumatic event

4. conduct disturbances, including problems that occur at home or at school that serve as responses to anxiety and frustration

5. doubts about the self, including comments about body confusion, self-worth, and desire for withdrawal (p. 88)

These indicators were specified by Fredrick to refer to young

children, but they are not age-exclusive. This author's expe
with acting-out adolescents shows that these behaviors serv
as indicators of prior trauma among adolescents and as normal responses to retraumatization.

Fredrick includes both structured (directed) and unstructured
drawings in his assessment protocol as well as a traumatic theme
coloring book, which invites written comments about associated
feelings and events. The use of such props underscores the need for
innovative methods in both assessing and treating posttrauma children.

SHORT-TERM TREATMENT

Therapy is not a mechanical process. While some approaches are
more obviously suited to some clients or problems, ultimately there
are no formulas. Effective therapy is a function of the interaction
between therapist and client. Just as clients have particular needs,
therapists have individual strengths and styles. A therapeutic approach that works well between a particular therapist and client
may be ineffective between the client and a different therapist. The
best choice of therapy takes such differences into consideration.
Therapeutic strategies, methods, and procedures cannot be chosen
without reference to the individual situation.

Within these parameters, however, some treatment considerations may be generalized. Treatment of traumatized children
follows and facilitates the general process of adjustment to trauma
spelled out in Chapter II in the discussion of work by Horowitz and
Solomon (1975, 1978). The initial factors in determining treatment
approach are the length of time since the trauma and the severity
of symptoms. This section will elaborate on this approach.

Treatment intervention considerations for children must differentiate between immediate, acute-stage interventions and
longer-term interventions. In general, treatment during the acute
stage with children should follow a crisis intervention model
(Aguilera & Messick, 1982). The object of crisis intervention is to
restore the victim to previous levels of functioning. Reorganization
normally takes place after traumatic stress, and significant maladaptive reorganization can be precluded by effective intervention

(Golan, 1981). Also, emphasis should be placed upon mobilization of the individual's resources. In the case of traumatized children, this may include family intervention and assessment of the family's capability to provide the supportive environment the child needs at the time.

The goal of crisis intervention is the cessation of emergency reactions. Following a shared assessment of the personal situation, initial feelings and reactions are allowed and emotional support provided. The opportunity to talk, cry, express anger, or whatever else is provided. The initial desired outcome is the mobilization of the individual's personal, familial, and social resources for coping with the event. The emphasis is upon short-term goals, practical considerations, and concrete plans of action.

Crisis intervention with children provides an opportunity for children to make public their distress. Unlike crisis intervention with adults, this work with children requires extensive family involvement. A good conceptualization might be to apply the same sort of initial defusing of emotional content and reorganization of functions of daily living used with individuals to the family as a functioning unit. The child's dependence upon the family makes continued family functioning essential to the well-being of the child. The family is negatively affected by crisis affecting the child, and restoration of family functioning provides the support the child requires.

Jeffrey Mitchell of the University of Maryland Department of Emergency Health Services uses Critical Incident Stress Debriefing (CISD), a group crisis intervention model designed for traumatized emergency teams, that holds promise as a structured intervention approach with other traumatized groups, such as families. CISD follows a structured format and is employed as soon after the crisis event as possible (optimally within 24–72 hours). This process is described in Chapter III.

Not only do treatment situations arise in which individuals, children, and families are involved, but occasionally clinicians are faced with situations involving whole groups of people traumatized together. In long-term posttrauma groups, the basic dynamics of group management and process apply, with the commonality of theme and need for movement through the posttrauma assimilation process. With acute cases and cases following soon after the trauma, however, the clinical picture is different. In these contexts, the immediate need is for crisis intervention done within the group environment, using the same techniques as applied in individual crisis intervention. The focus is on sharing reactions, understanding the event that has transpired, restoring prior levels of functioning, and mobilizing traumas.

As mentioned earlier, the basic steps of Critical Incident Stress Debriefing and the usefulness of CISD in classroom traumatic incidents are discussed in Chapter III. The point to be made here is the importance of Mitchell's emphasis on a structural format to facilitate the group's transition through a shared process. Through implementation of group intervention for those traumatized, the cohesiveness of the group is maintained through the high-risk months following the incident.

While many have reported that a crisis "brought the group together," more often than not that is not the case. Groups tend to lose organization and cohesiveness when members have been traumatized together. The group process that Mitchell employs is instrumental on two counts. First, the effects of the trauma are moderated for the individuals involved. Second, the ability of the group to maintain its organizational functioning is increased.

Mitchell's Critical Incident Stress Debriefing model is applicable to the treatment of groups of children who have been through traumatic experiences together. Sibling groups of children who play together or children participating in activity groups are examples of natural groups who may undergo a shared traumatic experience. A more obvious and prevalent group would be the ordinary school classroom. The structure and trauma-appropriate format of Mitchell's model makes it ideal for clinicians working with whole classes or with other natural groups of children who were together prior to a critical incident and will remain together after it is over.

Crisis intervention approaches focus upon function restoration and initial work in understanding and expressing feelings about trauma. The aim is primarily crisis management; as such, while it is an integral part of posttraumatic care, crisis intervention is not intended to provide comprehensive treatment. More in-depth, long-term, posttraumatic intervention is required in assisting the process of assimilation and accommodation to trauma.

LONG-TERM TREATMENT

Long-term treatment refers to the purpose and intensity of therapeutic endeavors as much as to duration. Long-term treatment focuses on productive resolutions of psychological and behavioral issues and complications following traumatic experiences.

The purposes of treatment include symptom reduction (reduction of phobic reactions, sleep disorders, behavior problems, and so on), but ultimately treatment involves dealing with the experience of the trauma itself. Thus the clinical picture is generally complex and involves sorting through a number of intertwined issues. Some issues and complications, such as addiction, must be dealt with prior to approaching the trauma, while others, such as prolonged grieving, will not be resolved until the trauma is assimilated. In addition, some issues such as family relationships must be handled concurrently.

The central differences between acute and long-term intervention are associated symptomatology and resulting maladaptive coping patterns. Long-term posttraumatic interventions are discussed by Scurfield (1985), who outlines the following five treatment principles of PTSD. These principles are adaptable to child therapy, particularly in dealing with the family of a traumatized child.

1. Therapeutic Trust Relationship. Children and their families need to feel a trusting relationship with the therapist. Countertransference and authority issues can be particularly difficult with older children and adolescents. The therapist must be prepared to handle difficult information and emotions, and clinical skills in dealing with anger and grief are essential. The experience of trauma leaves difficult, painful memories and feelings of fear and low self-esteem. Frequently, traumatized persons do not feel good about how they handled themselves during the incident and afterward. Sharing memories and feelings about the event entails great risk and intimacy. Recounting the personal dimensions of the event opens the person to possible disapproval, rejection, or humiliation. Trust in the integrity, acceptance, and skill of the therapist is essential.

2. Education Regarding the Stress-Recovery Process. Because posttrauma situations requiring referral are often chaotic and seemingly out of control, children and their families need to gain a conceptual foothold. This includes learning facts and perspectives about what to expect during recovery. Especially crucial with children is that any concepts presented for educational purposes be understandable. The child's developmental level, conceptual processing style, and language skills must be considered when educational presentations are attempted. Readiness is a key issue, and timing is essential. Clinicians find themselves playing the role of teacher at various times during treatment. The use of stories, teaching tales, metaphors, suggestions, or handouts can augment direct answers to questions in presenting complex and detailed concepts.

3. Stress Management/Reduction. PTSD symptomatology can be mixed and functional difficulties varied. A hierarchy of treatment steps should be established, and the child assured that all symptoms will be dealt with in due course. The therapist should focus on coping strategies the child has used in the past and use those outcomes to assist the child to avoid maladaptive coping strategies. Specific problematic symptoms (such as intrusive imagery or loss of control) require specific techniques to alleviate the secondary anxiety and debilitation they can create. Various behavioral interventions can prove useful. Particularly useful in stress reduction is the approach utilized by Donald Meichenbaum (1983), called stress inoculation training (SIT), which provides a structural approach whereby the client is engaged as a participant in his or her own stress management. This, or a number of other stress management models, can be useful in teaching the client to monitor and control trauma-related stress problems.

4. Regression to or Reexperience of the Trauma. Basic in working through the traumatic experience is reexperiencing the event and uncovering associated submerged feelings. This process frequently involves moving back and forth between grief/sadness and anger/fear. The images and associations indelibly etched in the minds of those who have been traumatized are powerful. During crisis, people are highly suggestible, and the visual, auditory, tactile, and kinesthetic sensations received during the incident become associated with the emotional experience. As time passes, some specific memories are naturally defused of emotional content, while others intensify. To the extent the feelings and images become submerged, working through them becomes more difficult and more important. Until the event is "reexperienced," that is, until memories are brought to the surface and the emotional associations understood and put in perspective, progress toward assimilation and accommodation is stalled. Reexperiencing the event is central to the process of posttraumatic therapy. With children this process is moderated by developmental and conceptual variables; younger children tend to be less affected by "submerged feelings" and have difficulty conceptualizing subtle emotional differences, tending instead to evidence distress through somatic and behavioral means. Art and play therapeutic approaches tend to be useful with younger children, while role-play and Gestalt techniques can be added to the armamentarium of the older child's therapy.

5. Integration of the Trauma Experience. The event must be understood, its meanings explored, implications and changes caused by the event accepted, and acceptance of self accomplished (Scurfield, 1985, p. 241). Trauma precipitates a revaluation of the world. Given the event and subsequent life-situational changes, basic assumptions are sometimes felt to be no longer valid. These include assumptions about the extent to which the world is safe, what can be expected, whether or not to attach, who—if anyone—can be trusted, and whether or not life is worth living. Fundamental decisions are necessary regarding these and many other issues. Resolution of these issues is an involved process, but it is essential for the further optimal growth of the individual. The successful completion of future developmental tasks depends upon having a firm foundation. Fear or ambivalence in matters of attachment or value can undermine further attachment, commitment, or ability to risk.

The overall goal of therapy is to integrate traumatic experience so that the individual is free to develop in an optimal manner. This involves a basic restructuring of conceptual and perceptual functions to accommodate the event itself and the subsequent changes caused by the event. This integration and reorganization cannot take place until the emotional overload and oversensitivity surrounding memories of the event are released. Counterproductive coping strategies must be replaced by more effective stress management techniques; the individual must also understand the posttraumatic reaction in order to gain perspective and self-acceptance. Each of these tasks depends upon the establishment of a relationship of trust between therapist and client. When children are the clients this is of particular importance, because of their limited conceptual development, lack of life experience, and fragile concept of self.

Eth and Pynoos (1985c) discuss four common psychological methods children use to limit traumatic anxiety following a critical incident. These affect not only future functioning, but also the content of experiences worked through in treatment:

1. denial-in-fantasy (reversing the outcome to mitigate pain)

2. inhibition of spontaneous thought (to avoid reminders)

3. fixation to the trauma (unemotional, often incomplete, journalistic reiteration of the event in order to make it more tolerable)

4. fantasies of future harm (to avoid pain, memories are supplanted by new fears) (p. 25)

In addition, Lifton (1979) reports that where actions have been perceived as ineffectual, children engage in "inner plans of action" in order to undo harm or gain revenge. Again, it should be noted that these methods are not unique to children; due to the regressive nature of the posttraumatic reaction they may be evident in adults as well.

Finally, Eth and Pynoos (1985d) in their study of child witnesses to their parents' homicide, discuss the interaction of trauma and grief in childhood. When grief has not been processed because of a defensive coping maneuver that does not allow the withdrawal of attachment from the lost object, maladaptive behavior often occurs. The strategies designed to deal with the intensity of grief become symptomatic themselves. In order to overcome symptoms, the individual must accept the loss. This entails the following process:

> The child must first accept the loss through reality testing and then tolerate the experience of the pain of grief. The child may feel sad, angry, guilty, lonely, tired, confused, preoccupied, and perhaps even ill. The deceased will be remembered as the child struggles to adjust to the new environment. There follows the slow withdrawal of attachment to the deceased, increasing availability of psychic energy for forging new or stronger relations. (Eth & Pynoos, 1985d, p. 172)

When visual memories of the deceased cannot be reviewed and resorted, and when feelings toward the deceased cannot be explored, the grief process is blocked.

Trauma involves several elements that preclude grief processing. Eth and Pynoos (1985d) list five such elements:

1. Reminiscing may be inhibited because images of the trauma associated with memories of the person may interfere. The funeral, photographs, or compensatory play often assist in repairing the image of the deceased.

2. Feelings of guilt over conflicts in loyalty, accountability, and survival may inhibit grief processing. Inner plans of action to offset feelings of helplessness may result in self-blame.

3. Trauma can cause ego constriction when the child shuns intense emotion, narrows life choices, and develops cognitive difficulties. A cognitive style of forgetting may evolve.

4. Social stigma from the event may cause the family to respond by prohibiting reference to the person lost, which forces silence and blocks processing.

5. Finally, the traumatic memories can intensify fantasies of reunion and confound them with images of violence. This can make normal loss and related depression overwhelming and can result in helplessness (p. 175).

In the case of grief compounded by trauma, the traumatic anxiety and other symptoms must be dealt with first in order to allow grief processing to commence.

Because of the complexity of the therapeutic task and developmental considerations that require delicate therapeutic intervention, several approaches to posttraumatic therapy with children have evolved. The next section explores some of these approaches. This discussion is not intended to be definitive or comprehensive; it does not represent a "how-to" guide to therapy with children. Rather, it provides a general outline of the main features of each of several major treatment strategies.

THERAPEUTIC METHODS

What happens when a child is referred to a therapist? Different clinicians work with posttrauma children in different ways, mainly because clinicians differ widely in background skills and in preferences. Differences are also due to the unique characteristics of each client and each situation. But a third factor exists; simply put, a wide variety of therapeutic options will work. A thorough review of the variety of approaches and the efficiency and limitations of each would be beyond the scope of this volume, but some discussion about the variations in choices of therapies is helpful. Beyond indicating diversity, this discussion can indicate the manner in which each variation focuses upon some particular aspect of the assimilation/accommodation process. Thus several major clinical approaches to the treatment of posttraumatic symptoms in children will be briefly outlined, and some of the salient features of each will be highlighted.

PLAY THERAPY

Play therapy was originally developed to provide release of difficult emotions such as fear, pain, or aggression through the child's participation in play in the presence of a therapist. Its goal was insight and interpretation of experience. Originally quite structured, play therapy today is relatively unstructured and allows the child to set the limits of the play situation. Currently, play therapists vary in the extent to which the child defines the process, the types of toys used, the extent of adult involvement, and the extent to which play is utilized in the overall therapeutic approach. Further, many play therapists use psychoanalytic principles of defense mechanisms, the unconscious, resistance, transference, and countertransference to explain play.

Toys that can encourage communication may be used in several ways and are capable of eliciting aggressive responses. As the child plays with the toys in his or her own way, the therapist can respond to the feelings expressed, build an interactive relationship with the child, and gradually help the child understand and restructure behaviors around a particular problem.

Play can be structured by the therapist into a set of sequences encouraging the child to face and master areas of conflict in real life. The therapist must establish considerable rapport with the child prior to initiating such directive leadership, and must work at maintaining rapport by encouraging verbal elaboration and using the child's pacing as cues.

Gradually the trends and problems reflected in the play become the explicit focus of discussion, expression, and problem solving. Play therapy can be utilized for general, developmental issue-oriented counseling, or it can focus upon trauma- and post-trauma-specific issues. Myrich and Holdin (1971) describe this play process in therapy with three stages:

Stage 1. The therapist creates an open atmosphere without attempting to force specific themes, types of play, or types of toys. The goal is to build rapport between child and therapist and to give the child permission in freely exploring forms of play. The secondary goal during this stage is the assessment of the child's problems, characteristics, and strengths. The therapist develops hypotheses regarding the specific problem formation.

Stage 2. This stage begins when a relationship of rapport, caring, and trust exists between therapist and child. At this point, the therapist introduces toys and activities he or she believes (according to the hypothesis formulated) will elicit feelings, concepts, and communication related to the apparent problem area. The therapist notes reactions to these toys, and either considers the hypothesis supported or generates alternative hypotheses. Therapist and child discuss feelings, perceptions, and behaviors related to these toys and to the problem.

Stage 3. This is begun once the problem area is crystallized in the therapist's mind. This consists of a series of graduated play experiences designed to focus the child's activity directly on the issues at hand. This stage utilizes a desensitization process and brings the child's expressions of feelings and development of conceptual perspective to bear on the problem. Through the facilitation of expression, clarification of behaviors and situations, and assistance in problem solving, the child's ability to deal with the traumatic experience and changed life situation is enhanced.

Play therapy utilizes the natural medium of play to build a helping relationship between child and therapist and to explore the cognitive and affective dimensions of the child's experience.

ART THERAPY

Art therapies vary as widely as play therapies and can be said to have in common only the fact that visual and graphic materials are used to accomplish therapeutic ends. Art therapists have advocated the use of art as a total therapeutic treatment, as an adjunct treatment with limited objectives, or as an activity aimed only at "enrichment." Art therapy is used individually with patients, with groups of patients, and with families. Because of the intrinsic attraction artistic expression holds for children, it is well suited for use with children who have been traumatized.

Through artistic expression, therapists can establish accelerated rapport with children, gain access to complex conscious and unconscious material with minimum defensiveness, and provide opportunities for the expression of "unacceptable" feelings or truths. In addition, the content and process of artistic endeavor are useful diagnostically and provide corroborative evidence to substantiate information gained directly or indirectly elsewhere. Therapists need to have an understanding of children's developmental stages in drawing as well as some of the background of the child in order to make sense of the child's drawing diagnostically.

Kramer (1971) categorized five basic ways in which art materials can be used in therapy:

1. precursory activities: scribbling, smearing, exploring physical properties of the material in ways that do not lead to the creation of symbolic configurations but are experienced as positive and egosyntonic

2. chaotic discharge: spilling, splashing, pounding, and other destructive behaviors leading to loss of control

3. art in the service of defense: copying, tracing, banal conventional production, and stereotyped repetition

4. pictographs: pictorial communications that replace or supplement words (such communications occur as the therapeutic relationship grows)

5. formed expression: art in the full sense of the word—the production of symbolic configurations that successfully serve both self-expression and communication

The selection of materials, as well as activities, must take several factors into account. The age, developmental level, and dexterity of the child must be considered. Further, individuals vary as to the emotional reactions different media evoke.

Art therapists differ as to the basis for and importance of interpretation of form and content, and the art therapy literature provides a variety of interpretive schemes. As with any procedure that reveals partial information about the client, however, all such information must be treated as hypothetical until adequate corroborative evidence is available to justify working assumptions or conclusions.

The art therapist uses artistic media and activities to establish rapport, encourage communication, elicit themes, facilitate understanding, and promote the cognitive and emotional processing of children who have been disturbed by traumatic events. As in play therapy, the projection of and working with traumatic themes in the nondirective, supportive, and intrinsically attractive context offered by art therapy is useful in the treatment of traumatized children.

BEHAVIORAL THERAPIES

A number of techniques are included in the broad category of behavioral therapies. Generally, while art and play therapies use a projective and interactive approach in helping the child deal with traumatic memories and changed circumstances, behavioral therapies have traditionally focused upon treatment of specific symptomatology. Thus behavioral techniques might be used to treat posttraumatic behavioral disturbances, such as bed-wetting, phobic reactions, or school avoidance.

Behavioral therapies have been used extensively in the treatment of hyperactivity, phobias, low self-esteem, shyness, test and school anxiety, uncontrolled anger, disruptive and combative behavior, and sleep disturbances. A wide range of treatment options exists, including behavior modification, covert conditioning, relaxation and guided fantasy, hypnosis, shaping, modeling, behavioral contracts, and assertiveness training. Because the focus of behavioral therapy has traditionally been based on one of a variety of techniques to treat a particular symptom, a global behavioral approach to postcrisis treatment is not clearly defined.

Typically, behavioral strategies are employed by therapists in treating specific problematic symptoms within a more comprehensive approach for dealing with the overall effects of the trauma. Thus a therapist may use a play therapy approach in dealing with memories of the trauma, grief issues, and posttraumatic adjustment problems, but use relaxation, guided imagery, and systematic desensitization to treat specific trauma-related phobic reactions. The major value of this balance is that it combines and directs the effective techniques of behavioral therapy in an orchestrated approach that takes causal and underlying conditions into account.

FAMILY THERAPY

Play therapy and art therapy approaches to working with children were developed primarily for individual therapy, as were many behavioral techniques. These approaches have also been used within a problem-centered group format. In general, the same goals and techniques are utilized, albeit within the constraints of group interaction and relationships. Family therapy, however, presents a departure in focus.

Family therapists emphasize different aspects of family experience. Some use a psychoanalytic orientation, interpreting family behavior from an individual psychodynamic and object relations framework. Communications therapists analyze and intervene in the ways family members communicate with one another. Structuralists look at the power, distance, boundary, and coalition relations existing in the family and attempt to change family functioning in those areas. Whatever their differences, however, family therapists deal with the posttrauma child within the context of the family.

Family therapy does more than deal with family members individually or all together. Rather, the inspiration of family therapy lies in its ability to allow the therapist to perceive, interpret, conceptualize, and intervene with the individual, taking the family experience as fundamental to the life of the individual. Thus, while working with the family as a group is not only possible but preferable, working with the child individually takes family functioning into account as the child's primary shaping force.

The family of a traumatized child is in crisis. Whether the crisis occurred outside of the family or within it, the family itself is affected, and family experience and interactions will change as a result. A detailed analysis of how families react to crises and ways that therapists can best interact with those families is presented in Chapter V.

Family therapists deal with patterns of behavior within the family and between the family and the larger community. The therapist first learns to appreciate the realities and dynamics of family interaction, becoming a part of the life of the family. After conceptualizing how the family interacts in self-destructive ways, the therapist is able to initiate dysfunctional interactions, draw attention to them, and then present alternatives. Challenging such patterns, providing feedback about them, and initiating new forms of behavior allow the family to develop and practice options. Unbalancing rigid and limiting patterns of behavior, the therapist alternates between direct and indirect interventions. The therapist directly alters family interactions and regulates the emotional reactions of individuals as a result of those interactions. The therapist intervenes indirectly by providing feedback, interpretation, and conceptualization.

The goals of family intervention with the families of children in crisis are to restore family functioning to a level at which the child's needs for stability and security are being met and to assist the family in finding constructive ways to meet the challenge of conditions changed by the crisis event.

PSYCHIATRIC TREATMENT

Psychiatrists are medical doctors specially trained in the treatment of mental illness. Their training places them in a position to provide several services other therapists cannot. Psychiatrists frequently practice in hospital settings and often provide consultation to other therapists.

First, as medical doctors, psychiatrists can prescribe and supervise the use of medication. One argument for treatment that includes psychotropic drugs for symptom management is that trauma results in neurotransmitter changes in the brain, and medication can assist in rebalancing the neurochemical environment and relieve some of the overwhelming distress of the symptoms. This allows other therapeutic strategies to work. Psychiatric uses of medication include managing symptoms that are blocking therapeutic progress. For example, benzodiazepines have been prescribed for fear and insomnia, beta adrenergic blockers for physical symptoms of anxiety, tricyclic and monamine oxidase inhibitor (MAOI) antidepressants for major symptoms of PTSD. These medications have specific applicability and sometimes appreciable side effects (Eth, Randolf, & Brown, 1988). The use of medication in psychiatric treatment requires careful diagnosis, prescription, and monitoring.

Second, psychiatrists are highly trained in differential diagnosis and can be especially helpful in complex cases, distinguishing between symptoms specific to the trauma and those connected with other psychiatric conditions. These distinctions, often subtle, can provide critical directions for treatment. For instance, preexisting psychopathological conditions can predispose people to posttrauma symptoms, and can be exacerbated by psychosocial stressors (Eth et al., 1988). In addition, anxiety disorders, depressive disorders, or organic conditions can develop following and in addition to a trauma, further complicating the clinical picture (American Psychiatric Association, 1987).

Finally, psychiatrists can provide case management, orchestrating the efforts of several treatment disciplines for maximum effectiveness. This is particularly important in hospital settings, where the patient may be seeing psychologists for testing, art therapists, vocational rehabilitation counselors, physical therapists, and social workers in addition to being under medical supervision. This may occur outside the hospital as well. For example, a client may self-refer to a family therapist for a family problem. Observing some serious personal symptoms, the family therapist might begin family treatment and then make an additional referral to a psychiatrist for closer diagnosis, consideration of medication, and treatment consultation.

ADOLESCENT
TREATMENT CONSIDERATIONS

It is little more than an axiom in the therapy business that "what you see is rarely what you get." Presenting symptoms are not the whole problem, and even with suicidal behavior or drug addiction, treating the symptom is only the beginning. Most behavioral symptoms that generate referrals to mental health professionals are secondary to other deep-seated problems. This is particularly true with adolescents. Very few adolescents refer themselves to therapists; most are referred by school authorities, parents, or law enforcement agencies. Most are referred for school problems, substance abuse, depression, self-destructive behavior, or running away. And, as the research discussed in Chapter I and Appendix I clearly indicates, a large majority of these young people have histories of psychologically traumatic events. Effective treatment of their presenting symptoms requires addressing, and at least partially resolving, posttraumatic issues in most adolescents referred to therapists for nontrauma reasons.

As mentioned before, reactions to critical incidents often involve regressive features. For that reason, dealing with posttraumatic adolescents requires familiarity with all the child treatment considerations outlined above. In addition, treatment plans must consider the developmental implications of trauma discussed earlier. The remainder of this chapter discusses issues unique to adolescents, although much is applicable to adults as well.

The research reported in Appendix I shows that posttraumatic symptoms are manifested in adolescence primarily through maladaptive behaviors, such as substance abuse, running away from home, and serious school attendance problems. These behaviors are self-rewarding—at least in the short run—in terms of relief of anxiety, depression, and interpersonal conflict. For this reason they tend to become entrenched as psychologically addictive habits, as part of the social self, as a component of a complex of gradually restricted life options, and often as chemical dependencies. Treatment for these maladaptive behaviors must begin by controlling the immediate situation, whatever the etiological factors.

The results of this study show, however, in establishing the likelihood of traumatic precursors to maladaptive adolescent behaviors, that a comprehensive treatment plan must address possible underlying issues related to prior trauma. To the extent the maladaptive behavior is founded upon developmental issues raised by a traumatic experience in childhood, or upon associated factors, successful treatment of the problem behavior depends in part upon successful resolution and integration of the trauma.

Thus treatment of trauma-related maladaptive adolescent behavior must include trauma-specific intervention. Apart from other treatment aspects such as family or network intervention, the appropriate use of hospitalization, or psychopharmacological intervention, and apart from the specific treatment modality chosen, a comprehensive treatment program should include the following three elements.

1. Reliving

The client must relive the traumatic experience (in the sense of revisiting memories in as full detail as possible), paying particular attention to specific visual, auditory, olfactory, tactile, and kinesthetic memories. The client's memories of circumstances leading up to the event and just subsequent to the event are useful in filling out the context of the experience. Associated cognitive and emotional states need to be explored. What the client perceived must be seen in terms of his or her interpretations, understandings, and conclusions concerning what transpired. The meaning the child has subsequently made of the event will be, in part, a function of the child's cognitive experience during the event. Emotional states during the event also become associated with the perceptual experience. Recalling particular sensory data will likely call up emotions that have been bound up in the psychological representation. Perceptual memories are very powerful means of gaining access to the cognitive and emotional realities that must be processed in overcoming trauma-related behavioral problems. Thus reliving the event provides the material for therapeutic gain.

Once trust is established with a particular therapist, adolescents are often anxious to share their experiences. They may willingly relate events that have happened to them, frequently with enthusiasm. Their interpretations tend to attribute responsibility for their own behavior—however contributive—to the situation or to other individuals. Self-structure is frequently tenuous during adolescence, and responsibility or culpability can be overwhelming. The therapist's use of indirect statements ("Situations like that can be really tough") or statements embedded in generalizations ("I've known a lot of people in this sort of situation who have ended up angry at . . . ") can often facilitate ownership of memories or feelings.

2. Releasing

It is normal for feelings associated with the event to be "bound up" in complex specific memories of perceptions, interpretations, and sensory data. People resist experiencing pain, and memories of traumas are usually painful. Once the client recalls sensory data, his or her memories of feelings as well as current feelings regarding his or her posttrauma behavior, changed circumstances, and relationships will begin to surface. The client may see the therapist as an irritant, someone who is rocking the boat and "causing" the painful reopening of old wounds. The feelings, once tapped, may be released in an overwhelming flood or may come out painfully, in small spurts. The client may have to relive the event several times in order to achieve the release necessary for integration.

Adolescents are reluctant to show feelings that may erode another's estimation of them. Because they frequently are self-centered, adolescents have difficulty perceiving therapists as functionaries whose roles are simply to help them with these varying feelings. While adolescents may suffer great pain from behaviors that get them referred for therapy, their resistance to treatment is high because of their fear of the underlying feelings.

3. Reorganizing

As indicated before, the goal of posttrauma therapy is too often the assimilation of the traumatic experience and accommodation to the circumstances that have changed as a result of the event. This involves considerable personal reorganizing (or resorting). This process can involve changes in

1. basic cognitive sets used for interpreting the world and anticipating what can be expected from it

2. emotional reactions that were experienced during and following the event

3. attributions of responsibility and personal control over events; and

4. attitudes toward various persons, places, and events

This resorting process may be profound and may manifest itself in depressive behaviors. Further, this process takes on a developmental dimension, since it involves reconstructing the present based upon changed perceptions regarding the past.

Adolescents are particularly affected by this reorganization. They are in the natural developmental stage of letting go of their dependency upon the family, and are attempting to establish themselves as autonomous adults. As with toddlers, the issue of dependency looms large for adolescents and creates inner and interpersonal conflict. At the root of this conflict is a fundamental ambiguity: The drive toward independence violates the desire for protection within the context of the child's role within the family. Since the security of the past is forsaken, each attempt at independent decision making triggers an anxiety reaction. Conversely, any relaxation into old family role patterns triggers a sense of self-violation and is interpreted as retreat. Always difficult, even under "normal" circumstances, this developmental task is compounded by unresolved issues surrounding prior trauma.

Much of what adolescents must deal with concerns the process of gaining independence from family. This creates a difficulty because the issues evolving from the family are often of paramount importance, yet the adolescent frequently needs to engage in therapeutic growth apart from the family. With adolescents, treatment strategies must be utilized that allow for indirect focus on family dynamics. These might include the use of Gestalt techniques, psychodrama, role play, or other more active techniques. In any case, as the study reported in Appendix I has shown, the family structure compounds the effects of critical incidents, including those occurring outside the family. One technique for dealing with the family context—family mediation—is particularly useful when the family situation prevents work on trauma-specific symptoms. Posttraumatic intervention with adolescents proceeds in a patchwork fashion initially, presenting such conditions as self-destructive behaviors, running away or being thrown out of the home, or violence within the family. These conditions must be dealt with immediately in order to stabilize the situation. Once some stability is established, time can be gained to deal with underlying, trauma-specific issues.

FAMILY MEDIATION

One useful strategy for stabilizing chaotic home situations involves the therapist assuming the role of mediator within the family. Mediation is a form of family therapy best described as a family system crisis intervention. In order for mediation to be effective, several conditions about the purpose and manner in which it is conducted must be made clear to all parties. These include the following:

1. The therapist must shift from playing advocate to playing a more balanced, and unbiased, role.

2. The therapist's advance work with each party should include a clear problem statement, spelled out in specifics. Clear goal statements are necessary, and various possible trade-offs and contingencies should be explored. This not only assists the adolescent and parents in generating a more flexible set of options, it also allows the therapist to introduce an element of reality into each party's expectations. In addition, mediation provides the therapist with an opportunity to assess what each of the parties is up against in terms of attributes, emotional reactivity, and interaction patterns.

3. Mediation sessions should be issue-focused. The expression of anger, hurt, or resentment, for example, must be managed carefully. The point of mediation is not to work through feelings, but rather to make decisions regarding rules and end arrangements of living. Often feelings must be expressed in order for movement to occur, but the focus must always be task-oriented.

4. In their fight against themselves for independence, adolescents allow closeness with the therapist only when they perceive the therapist is on "their side" against the parents. The therapist's impartial role in mediation may appear to be a breach in the relationship between therapist and adolescent, making advance preparation necessary. Thorough discussion beforehand of this important role and debriefing afterward can prevent rupture of the therapeutic alliance. The same difficulty exists in gaining the trust of the parents. The adolescent's attempts at seeking independence can strain family ties to their limits. Parents often seek a therapist as a further ally in their desperate bid to reestablish control over the adolescent. If they feel the therapist is siding with the adolescent, they may be quick to discontinue therapy. Before the therapist attempts mediation, this issue must be raised and a thorough understanding of the implications of the unbiased role of the mediator reached.

5. Each session should begin with a definition of specific

problems to be addressed and with a clear statement of decisions made. All decisions should be action-specific, with criteria of success indicated clearly and written down. Subsequent sessions should assess how well previous agreements are working, with particular attention paid to the specificity of agreement.

6. During the sessions the mediator plays a directive role:

   a. stopping and commenting upon the process

   b. restating rules when necessary

   c. feeding back impressions regarding the way in which each party is facilitating or blocking progress toward agreement

   d. providing relevant information, resources, or alternatives; and

   e. terminating and rescheduling the session if it becomes counterproductive

7. In addition, the mediator separates the parties for individual conferences regarding both content and process of the session. This might be done to clarify issues, suggest strategies, or enforce rules of procedures. Timely separation can also defuse rising tempers or provide time for an overinvolved party to regain composure.

8. The mediator, upon agreement of all parties, can include in the session other individuals who could provide helpful information, such as police officers, social workers, school officials, or other relatives. These people should be informed about the purpose of the meeting, their role, and the meeting format and procedures.

One of the results of initial mediation should be a decision about the circumstances under which additional mediation sessions can be called, and procedures set up to accomplish that. After the desired results are reached, mediation sessions are terminated. If the family so desires, family therapy can continue, but it will be under restructured conditions. Periodic follow-up sessions can be scheduled, and they should maintain the mediation format. The agreements reached should be monitored and adjustments made as needed.

Family mediation is a short-term intervention used to stabilize the family situation long enough for more traditional interventions to be used. While results can be revitalizing and transforming, the focus is upon stabilization. Treatment of the adolescent can proceed when the situation is stabilized, and the material presented during the mediation can figure heavily in subsequent work.

CONCLUSION

Therapists working with traumatized children draw upon two sources of specialized knowledge within their overall treatment strategy. First, they need to have a clear understanding not only of posttrauma reaction patterns, but also of the central tasks of posttrauma treatment. This perspective provides the direction and goals of therapy irrespective of clinical style or modality. The therapeutic "kernel" of reexperience, release, and reorganization focuses the basic task of posttraumatic therapy regardless of age. This task is accomplished in different ways by different therapists, and, of course, the choice of clinical approach is affected by therapist background, client needs, client developmental level, and the specifics of the situation.

Second, therapists draw upon certain specialized techniques within the context of their treatment plans. Formal approaches such as play or art therapy or family intervention may be used. Specific techniques such as the use of puppets, Gestalt techniques, hypnosis, or family mediation may be utilized within a particular approach. In this regard, the treatment of posttraumatic children does not differ all that much from other clinical pictures.

Other clinical factors may complicate treatment of trauma-specific symptoms. Family difficulties, running away, self-destructive behavior, substance addictions, and many other difficulties may require preliminary therapist-family interaction to stabilize the situation in order to make trauma-specific treatment possible. This is particularly the case with adolescents, whose resistance to therapy and reliance upon maladaptive coping patterns frequently create chaotic or life-threatening situations. Thus the therapist must be flexible and adept at designing multifaceted or even multiphased treatment plans with posttraumatic children.

This chapter, more a road map than a cookbook, has attempted to present these elements in a cohesive manner for the use of clinical professionals in order to provide a clear statement of clinical direction and an overview of therapeutic applications. Interested clinicians may consult Appendix II and the bibliography for further reference sources.

This chapter offers an outline of the overall task of the clinician in providing treatment. As such, it provides nontherapists an accessible explanation of what therapists do when they treat posttrauma children and adolescents who have been referred to them for treatment. Teachers, social workers, and church or other youth service workers frequently feel that all therapists do is sit and talk, or, conversely, that they work some sort of magic. This discussion is intended to provide nontherapists with a basic understanding of the optimal therapeutic process, so that they may have a clearer sense of when to refer a child for treatment and what to expect when they do so.

CHAPTER V

FAMILIES IN CRISIS

The "intrapsychic" realm becomes meaningless
if it is taken out of the realm of the relational
context.

Ivan Boszormenyi-Nagy & Geraldine Sparks
Invisible Loyalties

Accidents will happen in the best-regulated
families.

Charles Dickens, *David Copperfield*

The joys of parents are secret, as so are their
griefs and fears.

Francis Bacon, *Of Parents and Children*

OVERVIEW

*All professionals who deal with the families of children in crisis
deal with families in crisis. Whether the focus is upon the child, a
group in which the child plays a part, or the family itself, the professional's effectiveness will be directly affected by the reaction of
the family to the child's distress. This chapter provides a model for
understanding and anticipating the impact of the crisis upon the
family. The effects of crisis upon the central dynamics of family
functioning are discussed, as are the resulting potential pitfalls
for involved professionals. The chapter concludes by outlining
troubleshooting strategies.*

CHAPTER CONTENTS:

THE FAMILY'S RESPONSE TO CRISIS

IMPACT ON PROCESS DYNAMICS
  *Contractual Disputes—Role Rigidity—Homeostatic
  Resistance—Distance Polarity*

IMPACT ON CONTENT DYNAMICS

TROUBLESHOOTING STRATEGIES FOR PROFESSIONALS

CONCLUSION

HANGING FROM THE CEILING of the east wing of the National Gallery, the enormous but ethereally graceful Calder Mobile slowly swings around, constantly changing position. With its many parts linked together, the mobile nevertheless maintains a delicate balance, as movement is met by countermovement. Silently this massive work of art reveals combination after combination of spatial interrelationships as it dances through time. Families, too, change gradually, although not so silently.

As individuals change, other family members gradually adopt new roles and new forms of interaction; thus the family, like the Calder Mobile, adapts to the changing realities of individual movement and growth. The impact of crisis, however, can throw off the balance and smooth workings of even the strongest family.

Crisis can occur within the family itself. Some examples of internal crises include the disclosure of incest, the death of a family member, or an outside event that has affected all members together. On the other hand, crises may directly affect one member outside of the family; for example, a child may be victimized or may undergo a critical incident at school. In any case, the entire family will become involved. Educators, therapists, and other professionals dealing with either the whole family or children who have been through traumatic experiences outside will necessarily have to deal with the family on an ongoing basis. The professional's understanding of the dynamics of family functioning after a crisis will determine his or her ability to interact with the family in an effective, productive manner.

THE FAMILY'S RESPONSE TO CRISIS

Crisis puts great stress upon the family, interrupting routines, making abrupt changes, and creating much anxiety. Whether the crisis occurs within the family itself or affects a single member outside the family, all members undergo change to a greater or lesser degree. Change creates stress for the system as well as for the individuals within the system. Communication patterns, role relationships, expectations for each other's behavior, trust that others will meet one's own needs as usual, and flexibility in tolerating individual needs are just some of the affected dimensions of the system.

Just as individuals react to the stress brought on by trauma, so do families react. Family functioning adjusts in many ways to the changes within and between members. These changes can be for the better; often a family will respond to a crisis by drawing closer together, reassessing how it functions, and wanting positive changes for the enrichment of all concerned. Unfortunately, that is not always the case.

Often, crisis brings the opposite reaction. Families sometimes become fragmented, with members becoming isolated and unable to reestablish a closeness they desire. Communication lines can become blocked and resentments can develop that are difficult to overcome. Crisis frequently brings long-standing conflicts into the open in such a way that they may seem impossible to resolve. Families sometimes lack the resources to manage the restructuring necessary to accommodate the changes brought about by crisis.

This restructuring often occurs in three stages:

1. Recoil. Following a critical incident, family members initially respond by allying themselves to meet the threat. During this time the family feels closer together than ever. Almost a second honeymoon for the family, this initial stage is characterized by increased intimacy, trust, and communication. Long-standing conflicts and resentments are typically held in temporary abeyance.

2. Reorganization. Later, when the situation has stabilized somewhat, old patterns of communication and old conflicts and role relationships reassert themselves in the face of the increased stress caused by the crisis. This may lead to increased polarization, differentiation, and fragmentation, felt doubly hard by family members who have not only been hurt by the trauma but also feel new levels of isolation highlighted by the recent increase in family solidarity.

3. Restabilization. Finally, if family members are unable to rebuild the relationships exactly as before, the system settles into a new period of stability characterized by deteriorated or increased levels of intimacy, affection, communication, and trust.

As indicated, the reorganization phase presents a challenge to the family. New levels of family strength can be gained, or existing strength can be lost. Each of the process and content functions of the family can be explored in terms of the postcrisis reactions. An understanding of the specific challenge faced by the family following a child's trauma provides the professional a focus for intervention with the traumatized child and his or her family. The challenges of reorganization also present potential pitfalls for intervening professionals.

IMPACT ON PROCESS DYNAMICS

Process dynamics refers to the ways in which the family gets things done. How the family makes decisions and communicates, the

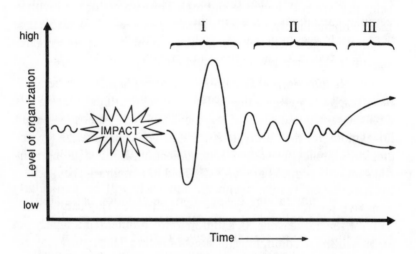

Figure 1. Stages of posttrauma restructuring. I = Recoil. II = Reorganization. III = Restabilization.

operational agreements and expectations, emotional distance between family members, how the family handles changes—all of these are part of the family process dynamics. Many of these dimensions of familyfunctioning can be affected by crisis and can provide challenges for professionals attempting to provide assistance. The most troubling of such dynamics can be contractual disputes, role rigidity, homeostatic resistance, and distance polarity.

CONTRACTUAL DISPUTES

Relationships are agreements. The contractual agreements holding within a healthy family provide efficiency, stability, and reliability in the ongoing coordination of family interaction. Confusion, resentment, and betrayal result from the unclear and dysfunctional contracts in a less healthy family. Crisis can focus family members' attention on their contracted agreements, allowing them the chance to restructure their relationship for greater adaptability, coordination, and intimacy. On the other hand, the crisis situation can stress relational contracts to the breaking point.

Professionals are affected by family contracts in two ways. First, the professional is thrust into a web of reciprocal expectations that are both invisible and real. Through his or her involvement with the family, the family structure changes, and the balance requires readjustment. Children have certain expectations regarding adult behavior, boundaries, and territory, and the intrusion of an outside professional into the family system throws their expectations into question. All necessary routines of family life are premised upon expectations regarding roles, rules, and standards. Most of these reciprocal expectations are unspoken, so the incoming professional must be alert for indirect signs of agreements and expectations among family members. The crisis situation probably has shaken family members, and each will be particularly sensitive regarding expectations for the future. This can be difficult for several reasons. In addition to the problem of a family not being willing to communicate "how things are," the family may not be aware that things could actually be different, or that the professional does not immediately understand all that needs to be known about the family.

Second, and potentially more troublesome, the professional may not be able to overcome his or her own particular family background and may proceed blindly, assuming that the client family functions just like the family back home. These perceptual "blinders" render the professional ineffective in dealing with new realities. Insensitive stumbling over personal territories, blundering into areas "not discussed," and violations of authority structures can cause great turmoil for the family seeking to reestablish order in their world.

ROLE RIGIDITY

A healthy family is characterized by functional roles. Each member has a certain amount of flexibility in changing role expectations and adopting new role functions when appropriate to changing situations or emerging personal needs. An unhealthy family is characterized by rigid, unbending role expectations. Under the increased stress of posttraumatic situations, some families attempt to cope with changes by controlling a family member's behavior. Limiting acceptable actions to established role-compatible behavior lends predictability and constancy to family interaction. This strategy creates difficulty, however, when the situation requires new means of coping or when individual needs have been changed by the traumatic experience. Role rigidity can be dysfunctional in the face of changing needs. The following case study is offered as illustration.

Case Study: Roxanne

Roxanne's mother had a certain amount of trouble with two things: men and alcohol. Her father was an alcoholic who left the family when Roxanne was very young. Her mother would go out drinking and pick up men to bring home, men who often became abusive and beat her and Roxanne. She finally found one she could beat up at least half the time, so Roxanne acquired a stepfather but retained the violence. Since Roxanne was the oldest child, she often found herself physically protecting her younger sister and brother.

Roxanne also did most of the cooking because her mother was frequently drunk or in the midst of conflicts. During her high school years, Roxanne worked after school and bought groceries with her paycheck. She cooked and washed clothes for her siblings and stepfather, and she broke up fights. Over time she became the family organizer, without whom the family would cease to run.

A crisis came when Roxanne decided that she could no longer keep up those responsibilities and still pursue a life of her own. Her mother and stepfather had separated and her mother had moved. Roxanne took advantage of an opportunity to attend a training program in another part of the country. The external pressure from all family members for her to stay was intense. Her mother did not want her to leave because of the increased work load it would mean for her. Her siblings were terrified that they would not be taken care of. Worse, Roxanne herself felt severe guilt over leaving them behind and almost abandoned her training program midway through after receiving a set of frantic calls asking her to return.

She became worried later when she found out that her younger brother was starting to cook for the family and had just taken a part-time job after school. Roxanne had left the role, but the role remained.

When dealing with families, professionals confront a system of preexistent contractual and role relationships; this intrusion always causes readjustment stress. Much of the conflict that occurs in a family following such an intrusion can be traced to the process of modifying and restructuring role relationships.

Often when such conflict occurs, the professional is blamed for the changes and is resented by those whose lives have been altered. The family members may identify (however irrationally or unconsciously) the professional as the one somehow responsible for the change. Thus establishing warm, working relationships with all family members can prove to be a lengthy process for the professional.

Some conflicts between individuals may be the product of

role collision rather than personal differences. The professional can become entangled in these disputes, which involve the entire family system, not just the obvious participants. Sometimes, where divisions exist within the family, some family members assume that the role of the professional includes taking sides in a conflict. Other times, professionals encounter resistance from the family member who feels that his or her role as authority figure is threatened. When this occurs, other members may experience confusion about who will make decisions or whose judgment to trust.

Finally, the professional may have expectations regarding role distribution based upon his or her own family experience. In the client family, the gender, age, and sibling order may not yield the same role functions anticipated by the professional and may be experienced as somehow not feeling right. As a consequence, the professional may make assumptions and act upon expectations that are inappropriate.

HOMEOSTATIC RESISTANCE

Families have an innate tendency to resist change, and to a certain extent this is normal and healthy. It provides the stability needed to maintain family functioning through the inconsistencies of life. It can become a source of malfunctioning, however, if this homeostatic resistance sacrifices the family's flexibility and adaptability to changed conditions. Crisis situations are chaotic, and, in the family's attempt to continue functioning through the chaos, homeostatic resistance may become a problem rather than a solution. Like a rush of antibodies after exposure to an invading virus, various forms of homeostatic resistance can render the family paralyzed in the face of a need to change. Conversely, in other families, crisis will shake the family loose and allow homeostatic habits to be reexamined. New forms of adaptability can strengthen the family system.

Resistance to change is a normal and frequent aspect of family life. Homeostatic resistance tends to increase according to the degree of stress the family system is undergoing. Thus therapists and other family consultants rarely deal with families in which major change is not occurring (or adjustments to a previous change being made), and they often experience the effects of homeostasis. Unnecessary conflicts, divided loyalties, contractual misunderstandings, role adjustment problems, and behavioral difficulties are all ways in which homeostatic resistance to change can surface.

Case Study: The Williams Family

The Williams family came to the attention of the school counselor when the family began an anti-sex education campaign among other parents at the school of their handicapped child. During the ensuing meeting Don and Sarah Williams bitterly attacked the school's family life program on the grounds that it would likely "put ideas" into the head of their 15-year-old daughter, Cindy. They reasoned that, having been disabled following an accident and confined to a wheelchair, Cindy did not need to have such problems started.

Like most couples, Don and Sarah had fantasies of what their baby would be like. Those fantasies had not included a disability. When they discovered that Cindy was not the adolescent that they had expected, they had to make changes. They accomplished these changes over the years, gradually developing a life-style to meet their needs and their child's special needs. This family life-style was hard-won, and it was based upon Cindy being a perpetual child.

The Williamses were not ready for the major changes that lay ahead. In addition to her physical disabilities, Cindy was not ready to live without supervision, and the prospect of making a transition to meeting Cindy's adult needs was overwhelming to her parents. Sex education served as a rude reminder that Cindy was growing up, and the Williamses were not ready to accept that fact and all its implications.

Generally, resistance such as that shown by the Williamses is a response to fear of the unknown. Homeostasis can also be based on unresolved loss and its denial; the attempt to sabotage change may be an attempt to resurrect the past. On the other hand, the origins of family resistance may not be emotional at all, but may simply be based in the family's lack of alternatives.

DISTANCE POLARITY

Distance is an ambiguous term when referring to affection, intimacy, and influence; thus it covers the wide range between isolation and fusion. Too much distance is experienced as abandonment, while too little is experienced as suffocation. Crises can serve to reawaken the bonds of affection and communication among family members; the threat of loss of things dear, whether routines, presence of significant members, or a way of life, can serve as a reminder to complacent family members, as can the reexperiencing of cooperation and shared goals. Conversely, where habits and routines have disguised the gradual eroding of affection and increased the conflict between individuals, upset and changes may serve to highlight the distance that has developed. Particularly in situations where resentment already exists, this distance may never be bridged and may escalate family fragmentation.

Not only do families have pecking orders based upon power relationships, they also have a definite "social territory" system that regulates the distance between members. This territoriality serves to maintain appropriate distances between members, and it is enforced by the contracts, role relationships, and feedback systems of normal family interaction. Family structural changes (particularly the kind necessitating the aid of a professional) frequently alter the social territorial balance and distance relationships.

Case Study: The Brownes

The Brownes first contacted a counselor in the middle of the night. Mrs. Browne, in a desperate call, reported that her five children were at that very moment fistfighting in the street. Advised to order them in and to call the police if they refused, she agreed to bring in the family the next day for counseling.

Mr. Browne had died two years before, and Mrs. Browne was left with a 22-year-old (who was recently married), a 19-year-old (who would have gone to college had she not felt so needed at home), and a set of 15-year-old triplets. The triplets were treated as "the kids," while the 19-year-old was cast as a mini-parent.

Mrs. Browne spent much time in the session (and evidently at home as well) complaining about how hard she worked and what little appreciation she received. Home life was chaotic, with cooking and cleaning sporadic, discipline overreactive or nonexistent, and much conflict and fighting.

In spite of the obvious need for assistance in regaining order in her home, Mrs. Browne managed to sabotage most of the therapist's attempts to reconcile family differences. She would start and restart arguments, use therapy time to spotlight herself as the victim, and contradict trivial details when her daughters were trying to speak. In addition, she would resist attempts to remove the 22-year-old (married and living elsewhere but still intervening in family arguments) from the problem situations.

Mrs. Browne needed to maintain an atmosphere of crisis in the house. She had continual fighting, arguments, and conflict to occupy her waking hours. She had to keep the triplets in the role of children so that her role as mother remained intact. She needed to have the older daughters invested in family roles to prevent them from leaving. She did all of these things because she needed to deny the profound feelings of grief she felt over the death of her husband, a loss she had not yet accepted. The family was held in the grip of homeostatic paralysis until she could resolve that loss.

Professionals may violate family distance patterns without being aware of doing so. Because regulation mechanisms differ from family to family, professionals may fail to perceive these patterns because they are used to the ways their own families, or families with whom they have worked, operate. In addition, lack of awareness on the part of the professional of how certain patterns of interaction function to regulate distance within a particular family may result in missed communication from family to professional and distance violations by the professional, leading to further communication difficulties. Finally, unaware professionals may find themselves "triangled" into a family conflict, and consequently their efforts are rendered less effective.

The previously discussed process dimensions of the family

focused upon the manner in which crisis affects family functioning, particularly at the second stage of reaction. As the immediacy of the crisis is over and the normal family relationships confront the changed, postcrisis realities, the family system responds either positively or negatively in its coping strategies. Positive coping results in increasingly flexible and adaptive roles and contractual relationships, decreased homeostatic rigidity, and distance adjustments that are more nourishing for the development of the individuals within that family. If the system responds negatively, the family is pitched into role and contractual inflexibility and maladaptive retrenching. Homeostatic paralysis limits the family's adaptive capacity, and isolation and fragmentation ensue.

IMPACT ON CONTENT DYNAMICS

The content dimensions of family functioning reflect this vitalizing versus disintegrating effect of crisis on the family. The extent to which family members feel loved or unloved may be challenged by crisis reactions. Differences in perceptions of love and distinctions about which behaviors evidence love may become problematic as the process dimensions of family functioning reflect the stress of the crisis. Further, the bonds of love may be shown to be inadequate to counteract the debilitating effects of dysfunctional process—love may not be enough. Similarly, parenting style differences, likely minimized during the regular life of the family, may create serious conflict between the parents and confusion among the children in the chaotic postcrisis environment.

Like individuals, families differ from one another in the ways they show affection and the ways in which they expect affection to be shown to them. It is easy for a professional, caught in his or her own pattern of expectations, to misinterpret differences in family modes of loving as being lack of love. It may well be that in a particular family a child really is not loved or is not shown love appropriately, and the professional can help in that situation. However, the professional must take care to be sure that the problem is not simply his or her misunderstanding about a different mode of loving.

Parents often operate on several levels at once. When establishing goals, expectations, and standards regarding therapeutic services for their child, they function from a rational, problem-solving basis. Later, when observing or evaluating those services, they may operate from a very different mind-set, heavily influenced by family legacies and introjects that demand different standards from those previously agreed upon. The professional may then be surprised at the apparently inexplicable change in the parents' attitudes, as the professional's work is found unsatisfactory, inadequate, or unproductive. Worse, the professional may distrust his or her own abilities in such cases, believing messages implying incompetence from parents whose doubts originate in their own conflicts over values, styles, and expectations.

The intrafamily ledger of obligations and entitlements may be unbalanced by the events occurring during the crisis and by the changed situations following the crisis. This may be intensified by unspoken contractual differences between family members regarding just who is entitled to what and just what sorts of behaviors create what sorts of obligations. Also, the crisis situation may have created new pressures that cannot be tolerated by members who suddenly feel burdened by obligations created by the crisis situation. Such obligations may force that member to avoid dealing with the others to whom he or she feels indebted. Just as friendships are sometimes lost because of indebtedness, families can be similarly affected.

Finally, family legacies—the roles, scripts, and predictions assigned by the family to individual members—may be confirmed or challenged by the crisis experience. Take, for example, a family in which it is assumed that women are unable to handle emergencies. In such a family, the women may handle a crisis by falling apart simply because they are expected to do so. Also, the mere fact that an overwhelming crisis has occurred—a rape, for example—may confirm the legacy to the rest of the family. Conversely, if an emergency occurred to such a family and a woman turned out to play an indisputably strong role in resolving the crisis, the result might be confusion among other family members or within the woman herself. This confusion might cause family members to begin reassessing their basic fabric of legends, legacies, and scripts, and the sources of continuity and stability in family functioning. Again, the family may be challenged to grow and mature from this experience, or it may suffer a weakening of the bonds of family culture, leading to estrangement.

The professional does well to be aware of contradictory behavior that is an outgrowth of an interplay between past and future. Professionals should observe such confusing behavior when trying to differentiate when adults are acting from their rational, fully powered present from when they are acting from their allegiances to the past, attempting to recreate an at-home feeling by being true to values they learned long ago. Professionals also need to avoid being cast as a symbol of the present, because those who are allied with the past will then resist their most sincere efforts.

TROUBLESHOOTING STRATEGIES FOR PROFESSIONALS

The following troubleshooting questions are useful in assessing family functioning. When faced with a difficult family situation, the professional should ask him- or herself the following questions to assess posttraumatic family functioning:

1. What stage of posttraumatic adjustment—recoil, reorganization, restabilization—is the family in?

2. Has the family passed from one stage to the next? Does that account for their changing relationships with each other and with me?

3. If conflicts between family members or between the family and me exist, could differences and errors in assumptions about mutual expectations create these misunderstandings? Would clarifying or making those assumptions explicit assist the family? [If appropriate to a professional role]

4. [If the professional works for an agency] Would misunderstandings about the role and intentions of the agency account for the conflict between me and the family?

5. Are there unspoken or indirectly spoken messages about expectations that I am missing or misinterpreting?

6. Could the conflicts, whether or not a result of faulty contracts, have their basis in role expectations that are incompatible, misunderstood, or different now than they were before?

7. Could my own conflicts be the result of misunderstood role expectations?

8. Are there differences between the roles I expected (as a result of my own background) and the roles particular family members play? Am I sure that such differences do not underlie the difficulties?

9. Could the family's demonstrating unnecessary conflicts, divided loyalties, contractual misunderstandings, role adjustment problems, or behavioral difficulties be a means of resisting needed change? (Consider how the problem could function to avoid family change.)

10. [If the professional suspects such homeostatic resistance to change] Is the resistance a result of emotional causes or based simply upon a lack of alternative skills?

11. [If the professional is experiencing conflicts with certain family members] Have I observed the closeness/distance relationships and how they are maintained through communication feedback? Am I transgressing distance limits? Am I unaware of distance messages that affect family members?

12. Am I making accurate assumptions about individuals' distance needs and patterns and about their distance regulation mechanisms? Have distracting patterns changed since the crisis? Does that create individual needs that are currently not being met?

13. [If the professional is becoming entangled in a family conflict] Is there any indication that I am being "triangled" in by one of the members?

14. To what extent has the crisis strained the bonds of affection, disrupted normal parenting functions, and challenged scripts within the family?

15. Have I looked closely at my own affectional and affiliational needs to make sure that I am not projecting those needs in my assessment of the family?

16. Am I clear about my own value structure, so that I can avoid negative evaluation of the family on the basis of those values? Is my assessment of the family based on the extent to which their values contribute to the development and well-being of each member, not on whether they match mine? Have their values shifted as a result of the crisis?

17. Could the crisis experience have created confusion or challenge to the family in the areas of value introjects, projections of belief systems, obligations and entitlements? Could this confusion explain otherwise inexplicable behavior?

18. Might conflicts between me and family members be based on those dimensions considered above?

19. In assessing parenting skills, am I basing the evaluation upon my own bias about parenting styles? To what extent has the parenting style in the family changed or deteriorated since the crisis?

20. Are my strategies planned with attention to their likely effects upon the whole family system?

CONCLUSION

This chapter has highlighted ways in which families respond to crisis. Knowledge of the outlined dynamics provides professionals who are dealing with posttrauma children some conceptual tools necessary in understanding the families and gives some direction in working constructively with them. Each of the process and content functions of the family has been explored in terms of the strengthening or disintegrating effects of crisis on the family system. Educators, therapists, and consultants coming in contact with families of traumatized children or with families who have been traumatized from within must be alert to signs of the family's particular stage in response to the crisis and the manner in which the family functions along these various dimensions toward strength or disintegration.

CHAPTER VI

TRAUMA PREVENTION

> For every person who dies, there are at least two other people who are going to be hurt, be it a mother or father or just a person who was a best friend from when they were little kids.
>
> 14-year-old friend of a suicide victim
>
> Death and Emptiness are the firm ground upon which life walks.
>
> Alan Watts,
> *Cloud Hidden, Whereabouts Unknown*

OVERVIEW

School personnel, as well as consultants dealing with schools, are called upon to provide prevention programs in many areas of student safety. While crises are often unavoidable, traumatic reactions may often be preventable. This chapter offers a prevention curriculum that provides an inoculation effect for children. In addition, recognizing that professionals dealing with crisis are themselves at risk for burnout or trauma, the chapter addresses the issues of acute and chronic stress management. A brief section discusses special problems regarding suspicion and reporting of child sexual abuse.

CHAPTER CONTENTS:

ANALYZING NEEDS

NON-TRAUMA-SPECIFIC INSTRUCTION
Problem Solving—Support
Systems—Communication—Stress Management

TRAUMA-SPECIFIC INSTRUCTION
Basic Concepts—Sensitivity—Classroom Management—

Confidentiality—Disclosure

PREVENTING CHRONIC PROFESSIONAL STRESS
Stress Symptoms on the Job

MANAGING SITUATIONAL STRESS
Child Sexual Abuse—Managing Critical Incident Stress

CONCLUSION

THERE WILL ALWAYS BE TRAUMA in the lives of children. Death is a fact of life, as are myriad other losses. Regrettably, children will continue to be victimized, and families will continue to malfunction. While crises may not be eliminated altogether, proactive planning and preparation can reduce the damage they do. Crisis prevention prepares children for difficult events that may occur later. Learning experiences can be orchestrated within the child's home life and school curriculum to ready the child for challenges.

What facts and skills should children be taught now to protect them from the possible harm of unforeseen events that might occur later? How can we prepare children without teaching them to fear the future and to adopt defensive postures toward living? Which traumas should the child be prepared for and which ones left to chance? Although these questions are troublesome, they should not lead to paralysis. Children should be provided with two types of learning experiences. First, they need to develop a generic set of skills useful in coping with any sort of traumatic experience. Second, they need to know just what their own reactions to crisis might be and what reactions are normal.

The best way to determine which preparatory skills and learning experiences would be appropriate for a wide range of crisis experiences is to start with an analysis of children's needs during and shortly after critical events. This informal and summary analysis should focus upon children's reactions and the eventual outcome of the events as discussed in Chapter II, "Children's Reactions to Trauma." Children's acute situational reactions to crisis are themselves frightening and upsetting, and children may be negatively affected in several ways.

Crises are typically experienced as a feeling of being out of control—a time when the individual's capabilities and resources are overshadowed by the situation. During such incidents, individuals are highly suggestible. The event overwhelms the child, who in turn experiences fear, personal inadequacy, vulnerability, and dependence upon others. Because the child is increasingly impressionable during these experiences, he or she risks the secondary reactions of lowered self-esteem, feelings of powerlessness, and heightened levels of anxiety. This erosion of the child's self-confidence and feelings of self-worth results in the need for greater coping efforts and increases the risk of maladaptive behaviors.

The posttrauma cycle is a stress cycle (see Figure 2). Reactions to the crisis create greater stress, leading to symptomatic behavior. Lowered self-esteem and pervasive anxiety leads finally

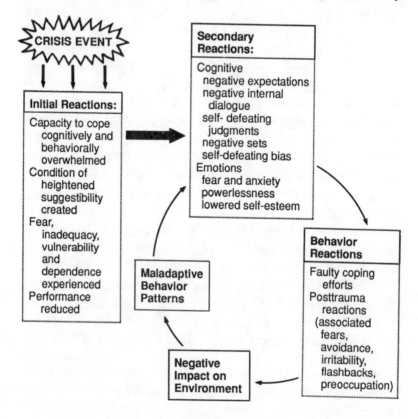

Figure 2. Posttrauma reaction cycle

to the development of maladaptive coping behaviors. Each stage is a response to the results of ineffective attempts to cope with stress. At each of the stages in the development of the cycle, however, effective stress management can interrupt the downward spiral. Stress management includes understanding not only the dynamics of the reactions but also specific strategies useful in breaking the stress cycle. If a child learns to use several coping strategies for managing reactions in stressful situations, those strategies can be transferred to crisis events. More important, if the child has learned which reactions are stress-related, he or she will be able to keep those reactions in perspective.

ANALYZING NEEDS

The crisis situation places intense demands upon the child's ability to communicate. Crisis creates personal and interpersonal chaos, overloading the child's capacity to organize perceptions, thoughts, and planning. This means that the child is frequently unable to determine *what* to communicate to others. The crisis situation is chaotic itself, with disruptions in routines, role relationships, and normal patterns of interaction. Adults are often as confused and disoriented as the children. Simple transactions and interactions become impossible, so the child is frequently unable to determine *how* to communicate to others. Yet while confusion and disorientation make communication difficult, the child's need to communicate is much greater than at normal times. The child needs to share emotional reactions and disorientation following a crisis with others to avoid isolation. He or she must ask questions to make sense of the situation. He or she must communicate basic needs. Most important, the ability of the child to work out successful coping strategies to deal with the posttraumatic reaction is dependent upon the child's ability to make needs known, to request assistance, and to stand up for his or her rights. This requires the ability to assert.

Times of crisis are times when people need each other. Emotional contact, understanding, sharing, passing information, and assistance of all types are just a few of the supports people in crisis need from those around them. The individual's total configuration of the people and the resources they can provide is called the support system.

During crisis, several factors conspire to render the individual's support system inadequate. First, people often limit their support groups to those resources they usually need; little thought is given to "what if" situations. Second, crisis sometimes involves the removal of a key person in one's support system, whether through death or through the person's involvement with the crisis. Third, the ability to conceptualize the changed support system and to fulfill those needs is often lacking. While crisis creates increased reliance upon the support system for continued functioning, the system is often deficient. Children, especially, have problems assessing their own support needs and determining how to get them met.

As indicated in Chapter II, many of the troublesome reactions to trauma are cognitive in nature. Children in crisis often appear overly calm because they are quietly struggling to make sense of the event. Reactions to difficult situations may include confusion and sensory overload, resulting in the inability to act effectively. Difficulty in distinguishing between trivial and important information and problems in setting priorities may lead people in crisis to behave in situationally inappropriate ways. Their time sense may be distorted; they may struggle to make sense out of incoming sensory data. These various cognitive reactions to crisis may persist for hours and days after the event and may become a problem. A child reacting to trauma may have great difficulty in basic decision making and problem solving. This difficulty will be compounded if the child is not skilled in decision making and problem solving. This deficiency leaves the traumatized child without the necessary resources to regroup cognitively.

Finally, following the trauma, the child may be upset by his or her reactions to the event. Cognitive disorientation, emotional upheaval, and physical symptomatology can be extremely frightening. The crisis situation is experienced as out of control, and then the child is confronted by experiencing him- or herself as out of control as well. This amounts to a retraumatization, and it often has as detrimental an effect upon the individual as the original trauma. The child doesn't understand that these reactions are essentially normal. The feelings, memories, and troublesome reactions attached to critical incidents are often experienced by children in isolation. Whatever adults know about the frequency of critical incidents or about normal cognitive, emotional, and physical reactions to them, children rarely are privy to such knowledge. Adults rarely talk about trauma with children. As a result, when experiencing a crisis they feel alone, and after reacting to the crisis, they don't understand their reactions.

This informal analysis indicates five postcrisis needs:

1. stress management skills

2. communication skills

3. skills in identifying and using support systems

4. problem-solving and decision-making skills

5. skill in understanding postcrisis reactions

Since prevention must consist of anticipating a crisis and then taking proactive steps to moderate the effects of the crisis, prevention efforts should focus upon these five areas. Taken together, the acquisition and understanding of these skills amount to a strengthening process, a development of inner resilience to stressors that cannot always be avoided. The first four needs are not trauma-specific. They are integral parts of any personal or character development program. They represent basic skills that facilitate attainment of personal life goals at any level. The fifth skill is trauma-specific. By avoiding the secondary response to crisis reactions, the damage done by the incident is minimized. A comprehensive prevention program includes concept and skills acquisition in each of these five areas. While it is beyond the scope and purpose of this chapter to provide a comprehensive discussion of each area, certain basic aspects of each can be outlined and salient directions defined.

NON-TRAUMA-SPECIFIC INSTRUCTION

The informal analysis of children's needs during and shortly after incidents has indicated five areas that need to be addressed in a comprehensive prevention program. One of these areas concerns the understanding of crisis reactions and is specific to traumatic situations, but four non-trauma-specific skills are also important: stress management, communication, support system building, and decision making/problem solving.

A variety of materials and programs already exist that stress a combination of such skills; a few of these programs are listed in Appendix II. Some programs consist of a "cookbook" of group exercises, others are primarily conceptional and theoretical, leaving classroom or group implementation up to the leader. Finally, some programs blend a conceptual direction with structural activities. Leaders are cautioned to have cohesive directions as well as flexibility in choosing and adopting activities to fit the particular developmental, background, and sophistication levels of the group. Children do need a focus, explanatory system, and sense of cohesiveness for what they are asked to do, particularly when they are developing skills in interpersonal contexts. Seemingly random activities that ask them to risk, stretch, and grow with no apparent reason or direction invite resistance. Children also need to be respected as individuals, with their personal differences taken into account. Groups will be more interactive and productive if the activities fit them rather than vice versa.

A complete prevention curriculum would be beyond the scope of this chapter. However, some general considerations that govern the selection of curricula are important. These considerations will apply whether the selection includes supplementary material, general approaches, or complete programs in any of the four areas. Thus each of the four areas will be treated separately, with general directions set forth to provide leaders with an overall "set" useful in curriculum planning.

One issue remains, however; should prevention material be kept separate, or should it be infused into the ongoing curriculum in the school setting? Abuse prevention trainer Wendy Deaton incorporates prevention into "in-place" curricula in her multidistrict program sponsored by the Richstone Family Center in Hawthorne, California. She advises teachers to take the following steps:

1. Use language and concepts that are age-appropriate. This ensures understanding and allows messages to be heard, not just said.

2. Support children's positive sense of self. Self-esteem is fragile, and often the first casualty of abusive situations.

3. Encourage children's freedom to question. This skill is essential to the prevention of abuse and other traumas. If the classroom process discourages the freedom to question, then the process invalidates its own content.

4. Recognize and label feelings. Feelings serve as indicators of inner and outer conditions. Children need to be able to identify and articulate their own feelings in order to understand what they are going through, to recognize when to take action, and to know what to communicate to those who can help.

5. Use games to develop problem-solving ability. Games provide a nonthreatening context in which confusion and difficulties can be encountered and solutions attempted. Talking about strategies does not aid learning as much as applying them under realistic conditions.

6. Reinforce positive ways of handling problems. Within the ongoing context of school projects and interaction, children should explore both positive and negative ways of handling problems. If positive approaches are rewarded they tend to become part of the child's permanent repertoire.

7. Develop positive communication skills. Communication, the foundation of coping skills, is necessary for children to enlist aid and overcome isolation.

8. Reinforce children's view of the teacher as a trusted adult to whom they can turn. This is the beginning of a support system.

9. Dispel myths about people, the world, or certain experiences. Often children act upon limited or faulty information and in so doing constrict their own options or act in counterproductive ways.

10. Utilize positive prevention materials (as opposed to "Don't do this!" or "Avoid that!"). Positive material pro-

motes strength and resilience rather than fear and de- fen-
siveness.

11. Incorporate entertainment and enjoyment to hold interest.
Children learn from play. Play is the primary means by
which children explore the world, attempt solutions, learn
from mistakes, and attempt novel responses. Capitalize on
this powerful force rather than fighting it.

12. Support assertiveness, independence, and autonomy.

PROBLEM SOLVING

Problem-solving and decision-making skills are essential for all
children. Growth is rarely easy. Children are like a myopic person
groping for his or her glasses in the morning; without vision, it is
difficult to find the right answers. Yet vision is a product of experience. In crisis the difficulties of growth are even greater due to
the abrupt changes, new and overwhelming information about the
world, the psyche's natural shock reaction to calamity, and increased stressors. When children are trying to cope with the chaos
of crisis or postcrisis situations, they need to have skills for solving problems and making decisions. Learning new skills in a crisis
environment is extremely difficult, and the situation deteriorates
for the child without those skills. When children have gained experience in decision making under conditions of uncertainty and
have learned a basic repertoire of problem-solving approaches,
they are in a much better position to minimize crisis damage. This
basic element of character development becomes the key in the
prevention of unnecessary psychological and physical harm during
crisis.

Most discussions of problem solving and decision making
emphasize the rational steps involved with evaluating alternative
courses of action. This typically involves some variation of the following six-step method:

1. Problem Clarification. Problem clarification not only involves a definition of the problem, but also rules out aspects of the
situation that are not a problem. Further, a clear understanding of
how the problem maintains itself and why it is a problem for the

individual is helpful, as is a statement of what sort of changes in the situation will constitute a solution.

2. Options and Alternatives. At this stage, various alternative solutions are generated. In order to encourage creative thinking, options should be raised whether or not they seem immediately promising. Once several options have been generated more elaboration can take place, with emphasis upon proactive considerations. The goal at this stage is to generate several well-formed solutions for possible consideration.

3. Evaluation. Each of the alternative solutions must be evaluated. The likely outcomes of the available options are compared with the changes in the situation as defined in Step 1. Each possible solution must be considered in terms of inherent defects, including difficulty in implementation and availability of resources. Any necessary preliminary testing should be undertaken and an open mind maintained in case new options present themselves.

4. Decision Making. If the individual is making a solo decision, this amounts to selecting which alternative maximizes benefits and limits liabilities. If a group is deciding, then the problem of consensus must be addressed. This may turn into a political conflict, so procedures for group decision making must be made explicit.

5. Implementation. The elaboration of options undertaken in Step 2 provides the groundwork for implementation. After the decision has been made, an implementation plan must be detailed and accepted. Four of the journalist's W's (who, what, where, and when) must be answered. The "why" has already been established. If an individual has decided upon a course of action, the plan of implementation may not need to be formalized or even recorded. If a group has made a decision, the plan will probably need to be made explicit. Part of a formal plan will include a time line and a system to ensure completion.

6. Evaluation. After the solution is implemented, the results must be evaluated. Did the results meet the needs and expectations that prompted it? Was the problem solved? Were the criteria for solution articulated in Step 1 met? During this process, new alternatives or even new perspectives on the problem may have presented themselves. The final evaluation may have shown the chosen solution to be deficient. In this case, new options can be attempted using the same steps. On the other hand, the solution may prove adequate.

This rational model of problem solving/decision making is presented in fairly full form. It can be presented in alternative ways, however, for different age groups. Young children may not be presented with this model directly. Instead, stories might be read or told to them in which problems are encountered and the children asked in a natural and conversational manner:

1. What's going on here?

2. Why is that a problem?

3. What do you think he/she should do?

4. What do you think would happen if he/she did that?

5. What else could he/she do?

6. Which do you think would be best?

7. What did he/she do?

8. What would you have done? Why?

In individual conferencing this model does not need to be presented directly. Rather, the elaborating questions could be asked and directed in such a manner as to engage the speaker in a rational problem-solving course.

The rational dimension to decision making and problem solving is not the only dimension, however. *How* decision making/problem solving is taught is just as important as *what* is taught. Learning increased autonomy is the content message of problem solving. That content message should not be violated by a teaching process that invalidates autonomy. Thus Deaton stresses a four-stage process with which the content can be taught in day-to-day classroom interaction. She presents this process for younger children, but it can be adapted for older children when appropriate.

In live problem-solving/decision-making situations, the adult moves through the following steps when the child is ready:

1. The adult makes decisions/solves problems, which the child observes.

2. The adult includes the child in decision-making and problem-solving responsibilities.

3. The child solves problems and makes decisions with observation and some guidance from the adult.

4. The child assumes decision-making and problem-solving responsibility, with an adult serving as a resource.

As Deaton points out, children learn best from modeling and experience; this format of gradual assumption of responsibility allows children the opportunity to evaluate information, recognize alternatives, and take action.

Another dimension of problem solving and decision making concerns the perception and evaluation of feelings. Because children often are taught to discount their feelings, they may confuse thoughts and feelings, ignore feelings as a valid source of inner information, and feel that their emotional reactions are of no importance. This leads to increased isolation and inability to communicate pain. As a *part* of the problem-solving and decision-making curriculum, the following steps should be taken:

1. validate and affirm the child's expression of feelings

2. assist the child in recognizing, identifying, and naming feelings

3. validate intuitive awareness

4. help the child to differentiate between thoughts and feelings

Decision making and problem solving, then, can be taught as a separate curriculum or infused as a supplement to in-place curriculum. In either case, not only should a concise problem-solving method be introduced, but the process dimensions of learning by doing and feelings as information should be stressed.

SUPPORT SYSTEMS

People need support from other people—emotional support, nurture, financial support, guidance, correction. Our normal life routines are carried out within a web of interdependence. People in crisis need more support. Crises deplete resources, alter the balance, create new needs. They can even change the available supports. Whether the crisis comes from within the group or family or from outside sources, existing interpersonal supports may be pushed to their limits and the supports themselves found to be inadequate. Children are especially vulnerable to crises, in part because they often lack the conceptual and emotional wherewithal to build, maintain, and restructure a support system.

There are two keys to an adequate support system. The first is the anticipation of need. Supports cannot be limited to present needs, and they cannot be limited to one's partner, parents, or family. When crises occur the personal situation changes and new needs arise, and this means that new supports must be sought. Yet during crisis the individual is usually the least able to assess personal needs, evaluate the types of support available, and embark upon a project to enlist the appropriate support. Crisis creates change; chaos creates vulnerability and helplessness. The time to engineer an adequate support system is before anything happens. This means assessing not only current needs but also anticipated needs during possible crises.

The second key to adequate support is an external system. This means that supports for one's family life need to include people outside the family. By the same token, supports for one's work life should include supports outside the workplace. Thus if the family or the workplace becomes the problem, the individual is not bereft of support. This is of particular importance for children, because the crises they experience frequently come from within the family, and the family is usually their primary source of support.

No one person or family can do all or be all for anyone else. The world is complex and individual needs are complex. The major content of support system curriculum lies in anticipating needs, locating people to meet those needs, clarifying what can be expected from those people, and learning how to access them.

Following are eight possible categories of support persons:

1. Leaders: These people can help by providing structure and direction. They can be especially important in the chaos following a trauma.

2. Guides: Although guides do not set structure, they do help define goals, consider possibilities, and think through positive and negative aspects of alternative courses of action.

3. Similar Souls: Such people share common interests, mind-sets, and concerns. They can help solve problems and motivate.

4. Close Friends: Close friends can provide nurturing, shared intimacy, and emotional support.

5. References: Often we need someone to vouch for our own character or skills.

6. Referral Agents: Agents can provide connections with other human resources.

7. Mentors: Mentors provide inside information, performance feedback, and motivation for a novice to explore new approaches and capabilities. Mentors may be abrasive or demanding.

8. Other Helpers: Other helpers can meet more specific needs, such as money, shelter, equipment, or safety.

With children, emphasis can be placed upon such institutional supports as police, medical personnel, teachers, and recreational leaders, and upon extended family care providers such as grandparents, aunts and uncles, or family friends.

The use and maintenance of a support system entails drawing upon people selectively as they are needed. This requires skill in choosing and in asking particular persons for assistance. Accessing support involves communicating needs and making requests (see the next section). Enlisting support also entails preventing those persons who are not helpful from getting in the way. In crisis, unhelpful social contacts are not supports. Finally, a formalized list of the system and how to reach the various supports is useful in assessing its completeness. Several operational rules are helpful in maintaining a support system:

1. Keep It Simple: An attempt should be made to keep the system as simple as possible to minimize the energy necessary to maintain it.

2. Keep It Current: The relationships should be kept up to date so that when support is needed the resources are informed and appreciative of the need for their assistance.

3. Keep It Equal: The relationship should be one that both parties feel is fair, whether this is accomplished by returning help, payment of money, joint sense of accomplishment, or whatever else makes sense. Otherwise resentment and guilt may build up and cloud things.

4. Keep It External to the Job or Family: The relationship should allow the person to engage in conflict or reorganization if necessary without undermining the needed support.

5. Keep It Flexible and Open: The relationship should provide backup support and feedback for the supporter, so that he or she can do a more efficient job.

The process of teaching about support systems may be presented in a group problem-solving mode. The group can brainstorm a great deal of the necessary information. One good approach is to begin by presenting a situational problem, then asking what needs a person in that situation might have. Once a set of categories is derived, then the question, "Where might the person go to meet those needs?" can be asked. Discussions may include maintenance questions and methods for requesting support. Finally, a rudimentary chart of each student's personal system may be made. The sophistication of the categories will be dependent upon the developmental level of the students, and the group discussions will generate an appropriately leveled chart. Such a chart should include phone numbers or locations if possible.

COMMUNICATION

In crisis, communication is the means through which solutions are suggested, decisions implemented, stressors changed, and support enlisted. Not an inborn gift or something that can be learned during crisis events, good communication requires skills, patterns, and intentional actions learned through practice.

Communication skills are taught daily in schools; organized communication skill activities and curricular material abound, and formal and informal instruction go on constantly. This is only in part intentional, because the majority of what parents, teachers, and other trainers teach children is what they do, not what they say. *How* adults communicate with children is much more important than *what* they communicate about. Some 75% of what adults need to teach children about communication is conveyed through how teachers look, dress, move, gesture, speak, and listen.

What the communication teacher *does* is most important. Teachers must model good communication by controlling nonverbal messages, saying what they mean, listening actively, asserting themselves, and letting others in on what they are thinking and feeling. Students learn to communicate by being taken seriously, by being drawn out, and by having their communications reinforced. Communication is two-way, especially in classroom situations; communicative teachers must interact in a real way.

Obvious ways in which communication teachers block communication and model blocking behaviors include the following:

1. Providing Solutions. Despite the efficiency of having the right answers, the act of providing a solution preempts the cognitive process of the solver, implies incompetence, and is an affront to the individual's dignity. Solutions should be provided only when the situational requirements for the answer outweigh the cost in terms of human autonomy.

2. Giving Advice. Related to providing solutions, giving advice implies a relationship of partial dependency and should be used only when adequate preparation has been made, ensuring that the individual is "ready" to hear the advice. Giving advice usually generates more resistance than compliance.

3. Preaching. Preaching and moralizing send an indirect message about the student implying a lack of trust in the individual's responsibility, moral sense, or ability to make personal decisions.

4. Warning or Commanding. Warning causes resentment, resistance, and rebellion, inviting testing of consequences and polarization.

5. Arguing. Arguing, or even attempts at persuasion through logic, provokes defensive positioning and counterargument. Again, the content of the message is lost to the process dimension.

6. Criticizing. Criticism, however well intended, is experienced as personal assault. Further communication is discouraged because attempts at communication expose the individual to social risk.

Since many of these blocks are practiced unconsciously, feedback regarding communication skills is essential to skill development. One very powerful format for teaching communication skills is triad grouping. Countless exercises can be carried out in groups of three. For most exercises, the three participants assume the roles of speaker, listener, and observer.

The speaker, who is following the directions of the exercise, is the active person, while the listener is the passive participant. This varies, of course, given the nature of the interaction required. For example, in tasks stressing active listening with a reluctant speaker, the listener may do more actual speaking than the speaker yet still be considered the listener because the focus of the exchange is to determine what the speaker is trying to say. The presence of an observer serves two functions. First, when exercises are conducted with large groups, pairs of participants can easily distract each other from the task at hand. The presence of an observer serves to reduce this tendency and to keep the triad focused on the exercise. Second, the observer can give valuable feedback to both speaker and listener as well as sharpen his or her own level of awareness.

Three areas that should always be covered when teaching communication are: nonverbal communication, listening skills, and assertion. In teaching adults nonverbal communication skills, the focus is upon controlling the messages sent nonverbally by the speaker, striving for congruity between the message and posture, gestures, and facial expressions. With children, however, the emphasis should be upon learning to "read" another's nonverbal messages. This provides the child with increased awareness and may help him or her in responding to adults during crisis situations.

This leads naturally to listening. During crises, children need to hear what they are told, particularly since their own ability to focus and understand is probably impaired. If children are taught to establish habits of checking out their understanding, asking questions for clarification, and eliciting elaboration until they feel satisfied that they really understand, they will be better able to seek the information they need when they need it. Once again, teachers can teach listening behavior best by modeling and reinforcing.

Listening includes focused inquiry. Table 3 illustrates the subtle differences in questioning strategies that can be modeled by communication teachers. They are grouped along two dimensions. The first dimension concerns the directness of the question, ranging from suggestive comments through facilitative questions to direct questions. The more direct the questions, the more confrontive they are.

The second dimension concerns the particular type of question and is divided between probes for content and probes for process. Content probes include the who, what, why, where, when, and how questions, focusing upon clarification, specification, and elaboration of detail. Process probes explore the implications of the content and the interaction itself. These include the feelings, relationships, impacts, changes, transfers, and choices following from the content of the message. Table 3 provides sample questions for illustrations.

Assertive communication is essential for children in crisis, who must make their needs known to adults around them. Because material is readily available for teaching assertion skills, assertiveness will not be discussed here except to comment upon congruity. As in other areas, the process of instruction cannot violate the principle or the content of instructions. Assertiveness cannot be taught without the child being allowed to assert him- or herself. Communication cannot be taught as a unit independent from the rest of the experience of schooling. If the classroom is managed so that children cannot practice assertiveness, character development requiring self-expression will be hampered.

Table 3: Focused Inquiry

	Suggestive	Facilitative	Directive
Probes for content			
Clarification	"Oh? ..." "...it did [or whatever appropriate verb]...?"	"In what way...?" "How?"	"I don't understand..." ask directly for deleted information
Specification	"...yes...[pause]" "this was..."	"Who [or what, when, where]?"	"Who [or what, when, where], specifically?"
Elaboration	pause, waiting expectantly... "...yes...?"	"...and...?" "...then what happened?"	"Could you tell me more?" "Would you elaborate more about...?"
Probes for process			
Feelings	convey empathy about expressions of feeling: "I think I might feel..."	"Sounds heavy [or sad, etc.]. Could you tell me more about how you feel?"	"How do you feel right now?" "Are you feeling...?"
Relationships	"Sometimes these things change how it is at home, or with our friends..."	"Is everything OK with...?" "How are things at home?"	"Do you feel OK about the two of us?" "Does ... believe you?"
Impact	"...wow!..." "...confusing?..."	"...sounds difficult [tough, painful, serious, etc.]..." "I wonder what that means...?"	"How important [serious, etc.] was that?" "What sense do you make of all this?"
Changes	"How are things going?" "...are other things OK?"	"Are things different for you now?" "Have you noticed other changes?"	"What about [mention changes you see and anticipate]?" "Any [specific changes you are looking for]?"
Transfer	"Sometimes there are similarities..." "Other things can get involved..."	"Are you seeing similarities?" "Is this affecting something else for you?"	"Sounds like...; what do you think?" "Does this mean that...?"
Choices	"...thought about what you might be able to do?" "Thought yet about what's next?"	"Do you have any options?" "Any plans yet?"	"What options do you have at this point?" "What are you going to do?"

STRESS MANAGEMENT

The final area of non-trauma-specific prevention curriculum is stress management. An extended discussion of both chronic and situational stress is provided later in this chapter. In general, children do not need to know a great deal about the theory or physiology of stress other than to recognize stress reactions when they occur. More important, children need to be presented with a range of coping strategies and enough practice so that they are able to implement those strategies themselves when necessary. Strategies useful in crisis situations can be addressed in trauma-specific instruction.

Two types of stress affect the child in crisis: background stress and trauma-specific stress. With background stress, children who are experiencing high levels of chronic stress in their daily lives or who have recently experienced other serious situational stressors are at risk for traumatization. Conversely, children whose lives are in a state of balance and equanimity are likely to be less seriously affected by a crisis event. Their psychological reserves are full; they are not "barely hanging on"—they have extra psychic energy to cope with the event. All children have stressors in their lives, and the manner in which they cope with those stressors determines their coping efficiency. Children who are not coping with their life stress well will have great difficulties handling crisis. Prevention programs should include components that teach children how to manage normal life stress.

The second type of stress affecting the child during crisis is trauma-specific stress. An overload of stress may be created by abrupt changes in routines and life circumstances, the entry or departure of significant relationships, or the sudden debunking of cherished assumptions about security and future options. Perhaps worse still, coping strategies that were adequate in precrisis circumstances may be quite lacking in the postcrisis environment. The child needs not only adequate coping strategies, but a reserve of future strategies, flexibility in adapting them, and the ability to access current functioning and coping skills.

The subject of chronic and acute stress management from the point of view of the working professional is discussed later in this chapter. Before determining specifics in stress management training for children, the reader should review that section. The various programs available in elementary or secondary stress management curriculum can then be reviewed for appropriation.

TRAUMA-SPECIFIC INSTRUCTION

The central focus of prevention is instruction in the structure of reactions to trauma. Stress management, communication, support system building, and decision-making and problem-solving skills are generalizable and transferable to almost any human endeavor. Noncrisis contexts such as social situations, school work, family interaction, and recreation draw heavily upon such skills. While essential to postcrisis stress management, they are not specific to these situations. Knowledge of posttrauma reactions, however, is specific to the posttrauma situation.

As indicated before, crises are compounded by the unanticipated emergence of postcrisis reactions. "Normal" reactions following crisis include various symptoms in each of four separate areas: cognitive, emotional, physical, and behavioral. In addition, reactions occurring during or shortly after a critical incident can differ from those occurring weeks, months, or years after the event.

Experiencing any of these symptoms can itself be disorienting, disturbing, and traumatic, particularly if the individual does not anticipate the experience. This retraumatization can be moderated and possibly altogether avoided if the individual knows in advance that such symptoms are a normal response to trauma. This can be accomplished through a structural preventive program stressing trauma-specific education. An adequate trauma-specific educational curriculum would include the concepts presented below, modified to fit the developmental levels and educational needs of the children involved.

BASIC CONCEPTS

1. Many experiences that could happen to anyone can be traumatic. These include accidents, death of parents or others who have been close, divorce, rape, bad drug experiences, assaults, abandonment, and natural disasters.

2. People differ in their vulnerability to trauma. Experiences not traumatic to some people may be traumatic to others.

3. Various background factors, such as those listed here, make some people more vulnerable than others to trauma:

   prior trauma
   psychological needs
   background stress
   physical fatigue
   family disruption
   recent changes or losses
   feelings of inadequacy
   overly optimistic or negative attitudes
   beliefs

4. Traumas may create various symptoms during or shortly after the crisis. These are, for the most part, normal; they include the following:

Cognitive	*Physical*
confusion	headaches
problem solving	pounding heart
difficulties	muffled hearing
problems separating	nausea
trivial from more	cramps
important things	sweating
time distortions	rapid breathing
	feeling of faintness
	other signs of shock

Emotional	*Behavioral*
fear	slowness
anxiety	aimless wandering
anger	dejection
irritability	memory problems
frustration	hysteria
	hyperactivity

Traumas may also create various symptoms in the weeks, months, or years following the crisis:

Cognitive	*Physical*
fear of going crazy	fatigue
preoccupation with incident	increased illness
orientation toward past	physical concerns
denial of importance of incident	
confusion	

Emotional	*Behavioral*
depression	substance abuse
grief	self-destructive behavior
guilt	sleep problems
resentment	social withdrawal
fear of reoccurrence	compulsive talking about event
over-sensitivity	avoidance of incident location
	school or work problems
	relationship or family problems
	flashbacks

5. Experiencing these symptoms means the event was serious, not that the person is crazy.

6. Normally, these symptoms initially get worse. It takes time before they get better. Talking about the incident and reacting with counselors, other adults, and even friends will help a great deal.

7. Some of these symptoms may never disappear, or long periods of time may go by and then suddenly symptoms may reappear. This is often related to stress or to developmental changes. When these symptoms are bothersome, it helps to let others know what is happening and to talk about reactions.

These basic messages, central to any trauma-specific prevention program, must be tailored to the group's developmental and experiential levels. The program must be flexible enough to allow for individuals to discuss their own experiences. Developmentally, some children are ready to deal with some subjects before others. For instance, 5-year-olds may talk about frightening experiences, accidents, or victimization, but they will not fully understand discussions regarding death, since their concepts of death are not yet comprehensive (see the discussion regarding loss in Chapter I).

SENSITIVITY

Professionals who lead prevention sessions must be sensitive to the possibility of trauma-specific discussion eliciting responses in children who have "unfinished business." Children who are especially quiet or distracted during the session may be having difficulty coping with painful memories or feelings about past experiences. The "right to pass" during such discussions must be announced beforehand and respected throughout. Dealing with such material is good if handled sensitively, but callous treatment of posttraumatic reactions amounts to retraumatization. Although it is tempting to use a group member's experience as an example when the child seems to be willing to discuss his or her experience, great care must be taken not to violate the child's integrity. When posttrauma individuals decide to take advantage of what seems to be a supportive environment to share their feelings and experiences, they are often acting upon impulse to break a painful silence. It is almost a compulsive act. When an insensitive or thoughtless leader capitalizes upon such a moment for curricular purposes, it amounts to manipulation. It is likely to push the individual to more disclosure than he or she may later feel comfortable with. This compounds the damage, discourages future trust, and reinforces the child's sense of isolation.

CLASSROOM MANAGEMENT

Classroom management during trauma-specific discussion can be a problem. On one hand, some students may become distracting and disruptive because the traumas from their pasts make the discussion very uncomfortable for them. Frightening images and memories, disturbing feelings, and difficult themes may arise in response to the content of discussions. On the other hand, the distractions and disruptions caused by such children may prevent other students who need exposure to the information from benefiting from the session. Although discussing trauma may be similar in some ways to teaching math, the feelings and needs involved are likely to be more intense. Often such situations can be best handled directly; for instance, the instructor may say, "Karen, you are doing [this] and [that], and that is disturbing others. Please don't." At other times an indirect approach is better: "A lot of people find that talk about [this subject] makes them nervous. Let's all take a deep breath and relax, and we'll try again."

Finally, when all else fails, the teacher may find it necessary to send the troublesome child on a special errand or task. In any case, professionals leading such sessions should always assume that disruptive behavior may be an indirect message, and should follow up with an individual conference. Chapter III discusses in depth how to handle such a conference.

CONFIDENTIALITY

Another sensitive issue is family privacy, an area that poses an unusual dilemma for which there are no easy answers. Children may need the opportunity to speak out about painful family experiences, but often families have informal and unspoken rules against divulging any information to others outside the family. This factor becomes extreme in pathological families, such as alcoholic, violent, or incestuous families. These families often actively enforce family secrets in order to prevent the children from disclosing to outsiders any details of the family's abusive behavior. If the prevention class reinforces this conspiracy of silence by not allowing children to speak about troublesome things, the isolation is compounded. However, no one wishes intimate facts regarding his or her life broadcast indiscriminately. Rules regarding group confidentiality are important but not foolproof. Such rules are only marginally enforceable. If a prevention session has 30 children participating, then 29 children from other families become privy to private information, as do their families, other children who are told, and the children's family friends, as well as the leader, colleagues of the leader, and their families and friends. Many parents become concerned when they feel that their child is being encouraged to tell family secrets during class or group sessions.

Thus the leader is again in something of a dilemma. If sharing personal stories is encouraged, the family's privacy may be violated. If sharing is discouraged, children's needs are neglected. While no simple answers exist, a few general considerations may be helpful:

1. Clear guidelines that address the right to pass, confidentiality, and ownership of feelings and perceptions can help set structure and positive tone.

2. A clear statement of the leader's own responsibility for reporting abuse or danger can establish parameters for discussion.

3. The leader can choose to make an explicit statement stating that students should respect their family's right to privacy. Students may be given alternative ways to discuss the issues, such as "I once knew of someone who ...," or "I have a friend who feels...."

4. The leader can model responsible ways to discuss personal experiences.

5. The leader should make certain that administrators affected are aware of the nature and process of the discussion, and should ask for their input on setting limits. Their support is essential in case of community repercussions.

6. The leader should be clear about personal comfort zones.

DISCLOSURE

In situations where traumas are discussed, the possibility of disclosure of child abuse increases. Children may say things in discussion that cause the leader to suspect abuse. Children may ask to speak with the leader after the session or the leader may wish to inquire further. In any case, where professionals have grounds to suspect child abuse, they probably have a legal responsibility to report those suspicions to proper authorities. Each state varies on liability in these cases, and it is essential for professionals to familiarize themselves with their legal responsibilities. Such liability can create anxiety and hesitancy on the part of professionals regarding their willingness to teach crisis prevention; this anxiety is normal and rational. However, those who work with children should keep in mind that thay have a moral responsibility, as helping professionals and as human beings, to do what they can to alleviate children's suffering. Therapists, school personnel, and others who work with children are often the only adults in a position to identify abused or neglected children and begin the process of social intervention. The best hope of such children is in the hands of those helping professionals with whom they come in regular contact.

Trauma-specific instruction, then, consists of both information and group affirmation, which function as inoculation against secondary reactions to crisis. Trauma creates isolation and the experience of being out of control. These feelings tend to undermine self-confidence and compound the effects of the trauma. Learning about the wide range of normal reactions to critical incidents is powerful affirmation to those children who have experienced crisis.

The next section presents a different perspective for the adult who deals with children's crises. As previously pointed out, the actions taken by an intervening adult with the child during or shortly after critical incidents can either compound the harm done or prevent further harm. One factor directly affecting an adult's ability to intervene effectively is the level of serious stress in his or her life. Stress limits the emotional reserves available to the professional asked to cope with children's crises. In addition, dealing with children's critical incidents can be highly stressful. Prevention must address the issues of chronic staff stress and staff response to crisis intervention.

PREVENTING CHRONIC PROFESSIONAL STRESS

Two types of stress affect a staff member's ability to manage crises effectively. The first type originates from the staff member's reaction to the crisis situation itself. This stress reaction will be discussed in the next section. One of the main variables determining the extent of the situational stress reaction, however, is the amount of chronic background stress the staff member has experienced prior to the crisis. Because background stress directly affects the professional's ability to manage children's crises and that, in turn, directly affects the outcome of the crises, an understanding of the management of professional stress is an essential part of crisis prevention.

Stress is the result of personal investment in difficult situations. If no investment exists, there is no basis for stress. Most professionals decide to work with children for all the right reasons. For the most part they like children, and they work with them because they feel it is important. Professionals who deal with children want to do the right things because they believe that what they do counts. They care, they are motivated, and they are set up for serious stress because of their motivation. Teachers, therapists, and other such professionals are expected to be the do-alls of society. Parents expect them to handle any situation and, worse yet, the professionals expect it of themselves. When stressful situations worsen, professionals often respond by increasing their own standards of performance. Thus the stress cycle escalates.

It is normal to assume that stressful situations directly cause our stress reactions. Yet investigations of the dynamics of stress-related problems show that they are best understood as unsuccessful coping cycles. Each stage is a reaction to the overall situation but also serves to set up the next stage. Because each stage represents an escalation of stress, adversely affecting the total situation, this process is cyclical in nature, as illustrated in this chapter.

The first stage consists of a situation and the individual's *expectations*. If the expectations are reasonable and realistic, there is a better chance of successful coping than if expectations are unrealistic and unreasonable.

The second stage consists of *appraisal*: the situation is evaluated for type and projected outcome. Three styles of appraisal can destine that situation to success or failure. First, certain types of judgments are self-defeating. Black-and-white thinking, preoccupation, categorical and absolutistic judgments, overgeneralizations, and "looking for the negative" can place the entire situation in an unworkable, pessimistic light. Second, a self-fulfilling bias may cause a person to concentrate on information that confirms preexisting beliefs and ignore information that contradicts those beliefs. The result is obvious—the person's subsequent experiences confirm the preexisting beliefs. Third, the appraisal stage may create stress due to a person's negative sets. Habitual beliefs, assumptions, and commitments influence the way one interprets situations. Past experiences and emotional vulnerabilities can lock people into negative ways of viewing and responding to the world.

An *internal dialogue* can serve to reinforce the negative appraisal and expectational set, compounding a person's reaction to perceived stressors. This is the third stage of the stress cycle. Not only does the person experience the world in a needlessly negative way, but he or she may repeat such self-messages as "Nothing ever goes right," "You blew it again," "You stupid fool," or "Oh no, here we go again" over and over again. Such thoughts happen almost spontaneously and influence the way a person interprets and predicts events. Negative thoughts automatically affect how individuals feel about situations and may create further negative situations.

The fourth stage of the stress cycle is *emotional response,* not only to the external events, but also to the expectations, appraisal, and automatic thoughts accompanying the events. When a person has perceived and appraised a situation as threatening and has listened to automatic thoughts giving negative messages, he or she tends to react emotionally, to get upset. His or her nervous system goes into the "fight or flight" response. This starts the complex physiological arousal process that leads to emergency behavior and further emotional upset.

The key to dealing with the emotional response to a stressful situation is to become aware of it and manage it before it becomes unmanageable. Early awareness buys time to change thought patterns, leave the situation, take action to change the situation, or work at modifying the physiological response itself. Physiologically, the relaxation response is incompatible with the arousal response, hence techniques that increase relaxation decrease emotionality. Getting away, controlling breathing, exercising, and counting to ten are active ways to break the stress response cycle.

The fifth stage of the stress cycle is the actual *response* to the situation. How a person responds in turn affects the situation positively or negatively. Responses are shaped by the appraisal, expectational, cognitive, and emotional processes in the overall interpretation of the event. To the extent those processes have been negative, a person is set up for a negative response. The resulting behaviors then contribute to a disintegrating situation.

A thorough assessment of stress reactions would need to include an assessment of each of the stress cycle stages discussed above.

STRESS SYMPTOMS ON THE JOB

Stress symptoms can be physiological, emotional, or relational within individuals. They can also affect a professional's job performance. Some occupational manifestations of stress include the following:

> work overload
> feelings of being overwhelmed by responsibilities
> inability to detach from work emotionally
> impaired performance
> withdrawal from or dehumanization of clients or students
> role strain
> decreased satisfaction

Teachers and other professionals will benefit by closely inspecting how stress is manifested in these ways and learning specific preventive measures to counteract and manage that stress.

Teachers seem to be one of the most highly stressed professional groups. In some ways their tasks are impossible. They must function at the intersection of a matrix of conflicting demands, and everything they do is a compromise between competing needs. At any given time they are expected to meet the widely diverse needs of a class of 25 to 30-some individuals. They are subject to the changing whims of parents, community groups, administrators, and legislators, and are expected to remedy not only educational but also emotional and social deficiencies. Moreover, teachers as a professional group seem to be more prone to self-criticism, perfectionistic self-demands, and sensitivity to criticism than other groups. As a result they tend to suffer from symptoms of chronic stress. Because of the paradigmatic nature of teacher stress, the rest of the discussion in this section will focus upon stress dimensions of teacher job performance.

Each of the occupational manifestations of stress listed above will be addressed, with a focus on how it affects the classroom teacher. Approaches to managing stress within the parameters of that manifestation will be discussed. Although specifically aimed at classroom teachers, it should be noted that this discussion may apply to any professional working in a human service capacity.

Work Overload

Parkinson's law applies to file cabinets and to teachers' work: It always expands to fit the space assigned to it. As if driven by a demon, teachers work feverishly at making work. If paper correcting is completed, then bulletin boards need revision. If that is done, then new assignments can be designed. If everything is in place and working fine, then a new system is necessary. While making professional salaries, most teachers take mountains of simple correcting home and do it themselves—a task that neighborhood junior high school talent could probably do faster for less than minimum wage. Teachers often lose track of what they should reasonably expect of themselves. They often adopt an "$n + 1$" criteria of acceptability. If n = a given level of their own productivity, $n + 1$ would be the level they would need to attain to be able to relax and be satisfied. Whatever their output, more is necessary. Few teachers would expect from others what they expect from themselves. This may reflect a "need to be needed," guilt over past "failures," or a need to be beyond reproach. Teachers—and other professionals—need to follow their own advice and set behavioral objectives for themselves, thus limiting their self-expectations. In addition, teachers rarely seek consultation. Teachers need to seek out others they can trust who can help them sort out reasonable professional expectations.

Overwhelming Responsibilities

Many of the same work overload dynamics apply to feelings of being overwhelmed by responsibilities. The specific job responsibilities as outlined on the employee's job description and contract rarely approach those assumed by teachers. As mentioned before, the teacher can choose to assume limitless responsibilities. The teaching situation is frequently open-ended, without objective feedback regarding the outcome of efforts expended in behalf of students. While test scores are limited to only the most clearly defined academic subjects, such as reading or math, teachers are tempted to look to newspapers, election results, and feedback from parents to determine how students are progressing in less tangible areas, such as values, art appreciation, literature, or character development. A sense of emergency exists regarding education on the national and local community levels, as journalists, politicians, and interest groups compete to address the latest "crisis in the schools."

Teachers need to step back and set their own teaching priorities. They should list the steps necessary to achieve these goals and check them off as they are completed. They should celebrate successes as they occur and acknowledge what has been completed rather than what remains. Teachers should also realize that the formation of a professional support system is essential for keeping one's workload in perspective.

Inability to Detach from Job

Teaching can be draining because lives are involved. Particular curriculum or class management problems can plague a teacher during off-hours. The plight of an individual child or family can seem insolvable. The burdens of overload and perceived responsibilities can weigh down teachers during the very time they should be recharging their batteries and revitalizing their lives. Teaching is similar to politics or the ministry; teachers are considered teachers 24 hours a day. Teachers don't have the social latitude that other nonprofessionals have. The psychological effect of working in a fishbowl environment reinforces the inability to detach. Teachers take their work home in their heads, if not under their arms, particularly when dealing with crisis situations. Knowing that individuals are vulnerable to both good and harm, teachers tend to take students' problems home and ruminate about them.

Overinvestment can produce worry or even cause the onset of a more serious stress reaction or burnout. A conscious effort to stop school thoughts at home, to leave preoccupation with student concerns at school, and to recognize when work life is intruding upon home life is essential to teachers' well-being. Creating and scheduling time for competing outside interests is not only valid but highly professional. Ensuring that family time gets priority is basic. Finally, if a teacher finds that concern over school matters becomes increasingly difficult to separate from personal life, time off may be necessary.

Overinvolvement with Students and Their Families

In college, teacher education students are instilled with humanitarian values and motivated to become personally involved in their students' lives. The virtues of the dedicated life are extolled, and the teachers-in-training internalize what they are taught. To some extent this is the best training possible, yet it can also be harmful.

While personal relationships with teachers may sometimes help students and their families and may certainly help to overcome the impersonality of the school environment, they can also seriously compromise professional effectiveness. Built-up resentments at nonreciprocal relationships and impaired judgments due to personal involvement may offset the gains that student/family rapport may bring. Psychologists point out that transference (unrealistically seeing another as someone he or she is not) can sabotage the well-intended relationship. For teachers, keeping professional role and responsibilities in mind is essential. Students in crisis and their families need help, and teachers are sometimes tempted to try to be the rescuer and fix the unfixable.

In such situations, teachers should remember three important points. First, the problem belongs with the student or the family, and not with the teacher. To the extent the teacher becomes enmeshed in the problem, the student loses one of his or her major resources—the teacher's professional perspective and objectivity. Second, the teacher must acknowledge that human beings have complex problems. With the possible exception of cases involving very young children and some cases of victimization, the solutions to those problems must to a certain extent be generated by the person with the problem. In the long run, the teacher not only *should* not but in truth *cannot* really fix anything. Third, depending on the extent to which the teacher's energies are sapped by overinvolvement with certain students, other students are deprived of his or her proper involvement.

Impaired Work Performance

Professionals are sensitive about their work performance and will be the last to admit impaired performance, even to themselves. *Burnout* is a term referring to a lapse in interest and motivation, decline in performance, and lowered professionalism. Burnout is a result of chronic stress or of overwhelming situational stress. A decline in work performance affects professional self-image and creates interpersonal difficulties on the job. Objective feedback is essential to teachers in monitoring their own personal work performance. This is true in many fields. For example, when asked about personal strategies for professional empowerment, one executive explained that he met every six months for professional feedback from another executive who had a similar placement in a complementary organization. The two men were in positions to observe each other's performance and were privy to gossip from the same professional community. Neither stood to gain or lose from the other's fortunes. Each benefited greatly from the informed, objective feedback. Teachers need to set up such sources of feedback for themselves.

Dehumanization of Students

Just as a nurse may refer to a patient as "the coronary in room 316" or "the appendectomy in 218," teachers often perceive and identify students in terms of their particular learning or behavioral quirks. Teachers find themselves seeing some students in terms of what they represent as obstacles in the teacher's day. Students become "class clowns," "problems," and "antagonists." A class of 34 individuals becomes 29 papers to grade, 5 make-ups to schedule, and

3 parents to deal with. The first-period class becomes the "easy" one, the second period class the "squirrelly" one, and so on. Student crises become entanglements to avoid—another burnout sign—that is often a precursor to decline in performance and professionalism. Time away from students often helps. Alternative, out-of-school interests that enrich professional or personal lives work wonders. Also, getting in touch with individual, successful, noncrisis students can revive optimism. If these strategies do not work and if consultation does not work, it may be time for a teacher to consider new career directions.

Role Strain

Roles are sets of expectations people hold about one another's behavior. When one individual fulfills several roles, different behaviors are expected of him or her. If incompatible or inconsistent behaviors occur, the resulting distress is called role strain. Teachers wear many hats (curriculum manager, disciplinarian, friend, team player, and more), and sometimes the role demands are ambiguous, conflicting, or ill defined. Role strain can be stressful, depending upon the degree of conflict and the degree of investment the teacher has in meeting all role demands equally well. Clarifying and setting priorities regarding role demands and open communication with other team members about mutual responsibilities can help bring an initial understanding of the situation. Additional perspective may be gained by consultation with other individuals outside of the school setting about the reasonableness of the various sets of expectations. Professionals may also seek support and out- side resources from other professionals. Teachers should keep abreast of changing expectations and revise their priorities accordingly.

Decreased Satisfaction

Too much drain for too long can make any well dry up. A teacher's energy and enthusiasm cannot be sustained in the face of a constant drain. When role strain, overinvolvement, inability to detach, and work overload begin to take the joy away from teaching, the result is dissatisfaction. Burned-out teachers do not gain a sense of satisfaction from their professional efforts or from themselves. When job roles become limiting due to specialization or increased role demands, new role responsibilities will usually revitalize flagging spirits. Doing research, joining an extra task team, or taking a leadership role may release energies that have been bottled up too long. Similarly, decreased job satisfaction may herald a need for outside sources of fulfillment or possibly reconsideration of present career directions.

Each of the manifestations of stress in the classroom discussed above can surface independently, but usually they come in a package. Also, teachers can take several specific actions to lower stress levels significantly. As indicated before, each stage leads to the next in an escalating cycle that tends to maintain itself. An adequate assessment of stress-inducing personal traits should be organized that takes into account the major stages of the stress cycle. Similarly, a personal stress management plan should indicate at least one specific strategy for each of the major stages in the cycle.

The discussion thus far has been limited to chronic stress within a classroom context, although it may be generalized to any human service situation. The stress reactions common to crisis situations with children have, however, not been addressed, and the next section outlines specific stress reactions common to professionals dealing with traumatized children.

MANAGING SITUATIONAL STRESS

Dealing with children's crises can be an enormously stressful experience for professionals. As one disaster psychologist commented after consulting on-scene following an airline crash, "One cannot walk through the aftermath of a disaster and remain unaffected." In part, perhaps because we as adults feel we should be able to prevent trauma from befalling children, dealing with children's crises takes an emotional toll. Since this helpless feeling affects professional performance, part of the prevention of further damage to children entails management of personal situational stress. This final section explores the normal reactions for professionals in crisis situations.

While we would like to feel competent in all things, able to walk through turmoil and difficulty unscathed, this rarely is the case. Most of us look back at our "finest hours" and either laugh or cry at how we felt at the time. It is normal to feel only marginally competent, only partly in control, and barely effective during a crisis. Usually only later do we decide that we really managed the situation fairly well.

Crises in the lives of children tend to engender certain types of unsettling feelings among professionals. Here are some common reactions to both individual and group crisis management situations.

Fear over Liabilities. When confronted with catastrophic situations, staff members often feel that they can do little to "fix" the pain. The expectation that "I should be able to fix it" leads to feelings of helplessness. Crisis situations sometimes involve specific actions that can be taken by professionals to reverse conditions, alleviate pain, or set in motion procedures for resolving problems. More often, however, there is little that can be done in this sense. Professionals often feel that they should be doing something more dramatic than taking the supportive steps outlined in this book. In part, this reflects a deeper feeling of despair over the human condition. It is simply one of the hard facts of life that people who don't deserve it sometimes get badly hurt.

Anger. Dealing with children in crisis is disturbing. Feelings of anger and rage are often the result of dealing with children who have been victimized by adults. When managing a crisis situation, it is important for professionals to take two steps: First, when interacting with others during and shortly after the incident, they should make a conscious effort to avoid displacing anger on others. Second, they should find someone to talk to after the incident in order to vent feelings of anger and gain perspective on the incident.

Guilt. Commonly, professionals feel guilt for not seeing the signs of crisis sooner or not acting sooner than they did. Related to this guilt is the unsettling feeling that if only one's training had been better or if only one had read certain books or if one had handled the incident better things might have been different. In the desire to protect children and act professionally there is a tendency to adopt perfectionistic standards in self-evaluation, often based on the fear of being evaluated negatively. While it is important to review performances mentally, at some point it is equally important to let go of self-criticism. Professionals must remember that reality will not be reversed by rumination.

Desire to Protect. Listening to the pain and learning about unfortunate situations often create a desire in professionals to provide 100% protection for the child 100% of the time. Obviously this cannot be, and usually the damage has already occurred. It may be helpful for those working with children in crisis to understand this feeling as a compensation for feelings of guilt, anger, or inadequacy.

Distrust. For the professional dealing with a traumatized child, feelings of distrust of the home situation, the law enforcement system, and the institutional helping system are natural. This distrust is further fed by the "what-if's." What if the perpetrator gets out, what if the police can't catch him or her, what if he or she gets a light sentence, what if the parents take it out on the child? It is difficult to determine who and what can be trusted when circumstances are chaotic. This may be partly due to the disorienting effects of the personal stress reaction. A good policy is to begin inquiring among other professionals working in the same area—"Have you ever had difficulty with...?" When such network investigations are not possible, direct confrontation with the agency representative or the person the professional doesn't trust is sometimes helpful—"There are some things which are worrying me, Mr....; frankly, I'm concerned that...."

Old Personal Issues. Often the child's critical incident or life situation parallels the adult's own past or present. While this can create shared experience, rapport, and understanding, it can also create discomfort, pain, and significant distraction. The adult's unfinished business can interfere with focusing on the student and can drain away needed energy. This occurs in several ways. The professional who is aware of the parallels and open to sharing them might become intrusive, spending more time and energy discussing his or her own situation than the child's. Such sharing can be useful in building rapport, facilitating sharing, or illustrating structural dynamics or solutions; but the adult will likely be hurting more than helping. When the professional is unaware of the parallels, he or she may be influenced by the personal unfinished business in uncontrolled ways. Thus decisions regarding the gravity of the situation, estimates of the impact on the child, and choices regarding what next steps are appropriate may be determined more by the adult's past than by the child's present.

Overinvolvement, unfinished business, or the intensity of the situation can leave the professional in great emotional turmoil, need, and self-doubt. Crisis prevention includes self-care to avoid difficulties later. Following a crisis management intervention, professionals should seek out social supports to discuss the event and explore the feelings the situation has raised, old or new. The perspective provided by an objective, concerned third person can be essential in managing the impact and subsequent effects of the event. If, during the crisis, the professional is unable to focus on the student because of personal emotional involvement, he or she should realize it and take care of him- or herself, finding someone else to take care of the child.

CHILD SEXUAL ABUSE

Of all the crises that can occur to children, child sexual abuse is often the most problematic to professionals. The situational stress reactions discussed above are intensified due to the nature of the offense. At the same time, there is an increased concern over professional liability, public exposure, and exaggerated media attention. These factors compound the already existing stress: The professional wants to help the child, but is afraid of the entanglement.

Sexual offenses perpetrated on children generate great animosity in adults. This is a deeply embedded reaction; most cultures have strong taboos against sex with children. This animosity is further compounded by recent revelations about the alarmingly high incidence of such contacts, further indicating that a great many professionals were themselves molested or abused as children. In turn, they are likely to experience intense feelings of their own when confronted with an abused child. The manipulative nature of the offense creates another source of intense reaction within professionals. Adults who molest children exert intolerable pressure upon those children to remain silent; they betray the trust children have a right to expect.

Professional liabilities regarding properly reporting cases of sexual abuse have become increasingly stressful. Most states and counties have very explicit laws requiring professionals to report cases of suspected child abuse to police or other law enforcement agencies, and professionals are legally liable if they do not do so. Yet, most professionals—even after specific training—feel confused about what does and does not constitute grounds for suspicion. Certainly direct disclosure counts, but the many possible indirect indicators are often baffling.

Against the legal and moral demands to report cases, some of which are not all that clear to begin with, is a set of threats to the professional who reports even clear cases. Professionals (sometimes justifiably) fear any or all of the following ramifications of reporting:

1. having to testify in court

2. lack of enforcement agency follow-up

3. retribution to the child

4. retribution to the professional, physical or otherwise

5. inappropriate removal of the child from his or her home and placement in an inadequate, poorly managed facility

6. lawsuits for improper reporting

7. overreaction by the system

8. disruption of school or therapy program for the child

9. retraumatization of the child

The family is a strongly protected, quasi-sacred social institution. Even an obviously dysfunctional family may exert political pressure on the school through the community. A professional who questions the integrity of a family frequently ends up isolated. The stringent requirements of reporting may leave the professional feeling that he or she has betrayed the child's trust. The powerful, often vicious, defensive reaction of the family may create a situation in which higher-level administrators or governing bodies will not support the reporting professional and will actually bring organizational pressure to bear on him or her.

But professionals must keep the larger perspective in mind. It is through public disclosure of child sexual abuse and involvement of many social agents that the abusive cycle is broken and the healing cycle begun. While it is tempting for professionals to view themselves as saviors working as solitary agents for children's well-being, the abusive cycle is too pervasive, too subtle, and too tenacious to be broken by one individual. The stresses encountered in combating abuse are best met in the same manner as the abuse itself—through a public, systematic approach that involves a network of support.

MANAGING CRITICAL INCIDENT STRESS

Child sexual abuse is only one of a host of critical incidents that can confront professionals working with children. Parental death, disfiguring accidents, and terminal illness are examples of other problems that can be overwhelmingly stressful to the professional who is attempting to deal constructively with a child. Like chronic stress, critical incident stress must be managed, or the professional will be rendered ineffective. Books, articles, workshops, and training programs abound with stress management theory and technique, and it would be needless duplication to outline such treatment here. There are several strategies central to managing critical incident stress, however, that would be most helpful to mention.

The first and most important thing a professional can do following a crisis incident is to go through a personal debriefing. The importance of this cannot be stressed too highly. Professionals need the chance to share their own reactions with others who are safe, who understand, and who are capable of dealing with the intensity of feelings generated by crisis. Ideally this should take place shortly after the crisis, but can occur with optimal results up to five days later. Background factors that set the stage for vulnerability to the incident must be examined. Personal interpretations of the incident that may be unproductive must be examined. Implications and meanings of the event must be explored. Feelings surrounding the crisis and personal crisis performance must be vented. Alternative ways of handling the emotional fallout must be found. The severity of the incident must be validated and personal adequacy affirmed. The most difficult part of this process for the professional is finding someone with the requisite skills whom he or she can trust. As a normal preventive step, any human services professional who deals with people should seek out such a person in advance and establish a working relationship with that person, so that he or she is available when necessary.

The second thing the professional must do after a crisis incident is find some other professional who knows of the situation and its context, someone who can provide perspective. This person can be approached for advice, clarification of perspectives, and presentation of options. This is a person with whom professional judgments can be verified and ideas considered. Such a relationship should not be contaminated with emotional overflow; consequently, this person should be different from the debriefer described above.

The third step is for the professional to determine the resources needed and available to handle the situation. These can include human, legal, material-informational, and political resources. The purpose of this assessment is to generate a plan for handling the emergency and for garnering the means necessary.

Finally, it is essential that the professional distance him- or herself from the situation. Professionals need to become involved in recreational, rejuvenating, and normalizing pursuits with people whose company they enjoy and who have nothing to do with the work situation in which the crisis occurred.

Combined with a rational, ongoing stress management program, following these four strategies in managing critical incident stress can do much toward diffusing the debilitating intensity of the experience. The most difficult part is overcoming the inertia and denial systems that bog down professionals following crisis. Having such a plan outlined and ready for personal use prior to crises can help the professional take the necessary steps.

CONCLUSION

Effective crisis prevention requires a multifaceted approach, including preparing children for crisis situations, preparing professionals to best meet the needs of the children in crisis, and managing the pre- and postcrisis stress reactions that critical incidents can intensify. Prevention must be proactive, and professionals must anticipate children's needs as well as their own. Steps should be taken in advance to meet those needs. And finally, as this book (and particularly the research reported in Appendix I) shows, prevention includes taking steps during and after critical incidents to moderate the effects of trauma in the lives of children.

AFTERWORD

THERE WILL ALWAYS BE CRISES IN THE LIVES OF CHILDREN, but whether or not those crises become traumatic depends in part upon the response of caring professionals. The first step in dealing with childhood crisis is prevention, starting with awareness of its frequency and manifestations. This knowledge includes the professional's awareness of his or her own history of personal crisis, and how that affects interpretation of and response to crisis in the lives of the children he or she serves. Thus prepared, the professional can begin to assess the needs of those children for prevention. As the last chapter indicated, children can be inoculated against the traumatic effects of crisis, through a proactive prevention program.

The second step in dealing with crisis is intervention. Concerned, aware crisis intervention has several dimensions. As Chapter III points out, intervention on an individual level differs from intervention on a group or class level. Crisis intervention skills and procedures on both those levels can be preplanned and provided in advance, before crisis strikes. Additional dimensions to be considered are the effects of crisis upon the family and the need to work with the family in providing appropriate help for the child. Chapter V discussed the family's reaction and suggested ways to approach the family constructively. Getting appropriate help for the family often involves referral to outside mental health professionals, and Chapter IV discussed not only the therapeutic process, but also ways in which educators and therapists can work together to complement what each other can offer the child.

The third step in crisis management concerns the staff. Airlines suggest to passengers that in the event of trouble, parents should first put on their own oxygen masks, and only then get oxygen to their children. It is a simple truth that an unconscious parent is of no use to a child in distress. The same holds for adults dealing with children in crisis. Administrators and support personnel must first take care of themselves to ensure their effectiveness in providing leadership and support to teachers. Teachers, in turn, must first take care of themselves in order to be able to care for their students. As the section in Chapter VI on managing critical incident stress pointed out, professionals can learn ways to protect themselves. Only then will they be in the position to deal with children's crises effectively.

This book has provided the background necessary for accomplishing each of these three steps. Its intent has been to arm professionals with the information, perspectives, and strategies with which they can prevent the seemingly inevitable crises suffered by children from becoming unnecessary trauma. What this book cannot provide, however, is the planning, policy making, and skills acquisition necessary for implementation. That can be done only in the field. That is the charge for, and the professional obligation of, the reader.

APPENDIX I

A FREQUENCY STUDY SHOWING THE CORRELATION BETWEEN CHILDHOOD TRAUMA AND MALADAPTIVE ADOLESCENT BEHAVIOR

UP UNTIL NOW, the problems of understanding and managing children in crisis (e.g., children who have suffered loss, victimization, or pathogenic family systems) and adolescents with maladaptive behavior problems (e.g., drug and alcohol abuse, suicidal behavior, running away, serious school attendance problems) have been treated separately in empirical research. If the association between children's crisis experiences and subsequent behavior problems in adolescence could be established, the effective management of both types of situations could be enhanced.

In order to establish the association between childhood critical incidents (CCIs) and maladaptive adolescent behaviors (MABs), 203 adolescents were surveyed, using questionnaires developed in conjunction with an advisory group of 30 student peers. Also, 4 adolescents were trained as peer testing assistants to help administer the questionnaires in order to minimize reactive effects toward the testing situation. A causal-comparative design was utilized to test two hypotheses: that there would be a significant and positive correlation between CCIs and MABs, and, second, that certain parental responses to children during crisis would have a moderating effect upon maladaptive behavioral outcomes.

Higher frequencies of CCIs were found to be significantly associated with higher frequencies of MABs; $F(2, 189) = 25.87$, $p<.001$. Adolescents who had experienced the greatest number of critical incidents also engaged in the greatest number of maladaptive behaviors. Additionally, adolescents' reports of their parents' responses during the crises were analyzed regarding their correlation with subsequent behavior. Parental response patterns were found to have a differential effect, with three patterns positively correlated with higher rates of MABs and one pattern associated with lower rates of MABs.

One-way ANOVAs were performed to determine whether parental response indexes (generated by a factor analysis of response items) were associated with differential levels of MABs. Adolescents reporting high levels of MABs tended to report their mothers adopting "withholding"($F[2, 185] = 6.5$, $p<.001$) or "inadequate" ($F[2, 185] = 12.80$, $p<.001$) response styles or their fathers adopting "reactive/escapist" ($F[2, 185] = 24.45$, $p<.001$) response styles. Conversely, students with low levels of MABs reported their fathers adopting "supportive" ($F[2, 185] = 2.98$, $p<.05$) response styles. An analogous positive effect, however, was not shown for mothers.

Data generated by this study indicate that childhood critical incidents may be strongly contributing factors to the development of maladaptive adolescent behavior. Further, this study indicates that parental response to the child during and shortly after the incident may significantly moderate the long-term effects of the crisis. Thus the present study sought to establish the general connection between antecedent events and subsequent maladaptive behaviors directly in addition to exploring the moderating effects of certain types of parental interventions.

NATURE OF THE STUDY

The study used the methodology of causal-comparative research (Isaac, 1971). Adolescents' maladaptive behaviors were examined in terms of both childhood critical incidents and parental interventions. The purpose was to discover the effects of past events.

SAMPLE SELECTION

The sample consisted of 203 adolescents from a relatively stable suburban community in Southern California. In order to reduce confounding variables, these were predominantly white, middle-class children, ages 15–17. Specifically, 133 subjects came from the community comprehensive high school, from five junior-senior-level English classes, including two advanced placement, three regular enrollment, and one lower-level placement. As all students must take English, this distribution was considered to result in a roughly representative sample of the student population at the school. Completing the sample were 70 continuation high school students of equivalent age from the same community. These students were included to ensure a sampling of chronic school attendance problems. (California operates special continuation high schools in each community for students seriously at risk of dropping out. These students characteristically have problems with attendance.)

These adolescents were queried as to their backgrounds, their history of critical incidents, the manner in which their parents or other significant adults responded to their crises, and their current behavior. Anonymous questionnaires were utilized for the reasons outlined below and were developed with the assistance of a panel of some 30 adolescents in order to maximize accessibility and relevance.

To minimize the reactive effects of perceived adult censure, male and female peer assistants were recruited to help administer the questionnaires and answer questions regarding item and procedural clarification. These experimental arrangements were adopted upon recommendation by the panel of peers, who were asked to comment on how the research could be done in a nonthreatening manner. It was felt that the above arrangements maximized the likelihood of sampling accurate information and minimized the possibility of reactive effects contaminating the data. The questionnaires were administered to whole classes to further minimize the pressure to withhold information, and names were not asked in order to guarantee anonymity.

HYPOTHESES

The following two hypotheses were tested by the study:

1. There will be a significant positive correlation between

childhood critical incidents and the frequency of subsequent maladaptive adolescent behaviors as measured by self-reports (on the Critical Life Events Survey and Current Maladaptive Adolescent Behavior Inventory).

2. There will be a significant positive correlation between the frequency of negative parental/adult responses to childhood critical incidents and the frequency of the children's subsequent maladaptive adolescent behaviors as measured by self-reports (on the Parental/Adult Response to Crisis Checklist and Current Maladaptive Adolescent Behavior Inventory).

DEFINITIONS

Childhood Critical Incident. Any psychological trauma in childhood which overwhelms the individual's capacity to cope.

Parental/Adult Response. Those communicative interactions occurring during or after a child's critical incident that are (or are perceived by the child to be) in response to that incident.

Maladaptive Adolescent Behaviors. Behaviors detrimental to the well-being of the adolescent; for the purpose of this study, the following will be considered MABs:

1. alcohol or other substance use

2. attempted suicide or suicidal ideation

3. running away

4. serious school non-attendance

Posttraumatic Stress Response. Response to critical incident occurring after exposure, including acute reaction immediately following the incident and delayed response occurring months or even years following the event.

Loss. A class of critical incidents including death of parent or other loved ones.

Victimization. A class of critical incidents including assault, rape.

Pathogenic Family Structure. Family relationships involving disturbed patterns of communication, coercive power distribution, inadequate resources, or antisocial values; critical incidents involving pathogenic family structure include incest, alcoholism, and parental fighting.

ASSUMPTIONS

The following assumptions provided the basis for the procedures used in this study and the interpretation of results.

1. Adolescents, if provided reasonable assurance of anonymity to avoid stigma or other consequences and if under minimum peer or adult pressure, can and will disclose truthful sensitive information about prior events and current behavior. While this is assumed, the rationale for adopting the specific instruments utilized to elicit this information is presented in the Limitations section below, under "Reactive Effects of Experimental Arrangements."

2. Maladaptive adolescent behaviors can best be understood as delayed stress responses to childhood critical incidents. This explanatory model, developed to account for adult disorders resulting from combat or catastrophe, has recently become part of the psychological lexicon. This model, placed in a child developmental context, provides the operational connection between past experiences and current behavior.

METHODOLOGY

This section is devoted to the methodology utilized in the study. First, the methodology will be described, and then the research design will be outlined, including specification of variables and the research hypotheses. Next, a pilot study will be reported. This is followed by an explanation of the instrumentation, including construction of the questionnaires. Procedures followed in the study will then be described, and the analysis of the data will be outlined. The limitations of the study will then be analyzed and evaluated.

DESCRIPTION

This study utilizes a causal-comparative methodology (Isaac, 1971), establishing relationships among independent, moderating, and dependent variables by ex post facto correlation.

RESEARCH DESIGN

Questionnaires were utilized to gather self-reports of adolescents' background experiences and current behaviors from a sample of 203 adolescents (see Sample Selection, above, for details). The variables are formulated as follows:

Independent Variables. Adolescents' self-reports of experiences during childhood that at the time overwhelmed their capacity to cope (childhood critical incidents), as indicated on a checksheet (the Critical Life Events Survey). Included are a wide range of such incidents (e.g., death of parent, sexual assault, divorce of parents, mental abuse) selected by a panel of 30 peers as being most critical. Space was provided for writing in repeats and events not listed. In addition, for each incident subjects indicated their age at the time, the severity of the incident, the degree to which they received support from their parents or other adults, and how stable the family was at the time. These latter factors can be treated as intervening variables (see below).

Intervening Variables. Self-reports of the responses parents and other significant adults made to subjects during and after their critical incidents were collected on the Parental/Adult Response to Crisis Checklist. The same panel of peers was convened to discuss and determine a range of possible responses. The ten responses deemed most helpful and the ten responses deemed most hurtful by the panel were then randomized on the checklist, and subjects indicated separately how each parent and one other significant adult responded to them during their worst critical incidents.

Dependent Variables. Maladaptive adolescent behaviors were sampled by self-report. MABs included serious school attendance problems, suicide ideation or attempts, drug and alcohol abuse, pregnancy, and running away. Serious school attendance was determined by enrollment at the continuation high school, as the predominant criterion for enrollment is a significant attendance problem at regular high school. Other maladaptive adolescent behaviors were sampled by self-reports on a checklist designed to maximize self-disclosure by being brief, anonymous, and matter-of-fact.

This study seeks to specify the relationships holding among these variables.

PILOT STUDY

The instruments utilized in this study (see next section) were pilot tested for adequacy of directions, clarity of questions and response procedures, and content concepts, as well as for administrative time. Subjects included those students who were initially used to construct the questionnaires. Through follow-up interviews, the instruments were evaluated and revisions made. The administrative procedure was formalized so that training of test administrators could begin.

INSTRUMENTATION

Researchers have generally supported self-reports as valid sources of data regarding sensitive issues (Gelles, 1978; Lourie, 1977). Adolescents, however, tend to either minimize or exaggerate their chemical use (Harris, 1980), so a data collection instrument that minimizes the interpersonal reaction effects of the testing situation was deemed necessary. Similarly, those exposed to victimization tend to underreport (Meizelman, 1978), so the same considerations applied regarding the need for anonymity in instrumentation.

The following instruments were utilized in the study:

1. Background and Current Status Questionnaire (BARC)

2. Current Maladaptive Adolescent Behavior Inventory (CMABI)

3. Critical Life Events Survey (CLES)

4. Parental/Adult Response to Crisis Checklist (PARC)

Copies of these four instruments appear at the end of this Appendix.

Due to its nature, this study required many data regarding previous experiences and current behavioral patterns. No existing tests that have been normed fit the requirements of this study. While some instruments concerning alcohol and drug use are available, they are far too long and cumbersome to be included in a test package without seriously compromising the student's ability to complete the testing. Instruments had to be designed, then, that could fit the demands of the test situation. Another requirement was that the tests had to be understandable to adolescents and sufficiently nonthreatening to encourage truthful responses. This section will detail the process by which these instruments were constructed. Considerations regarding validity of the instruments will be discussed in the section concerning threats to internal validity and in the section on methodological assumptions. Self-rating scales have been increasingly shown to be valid and reliable, and are currently widely used (Parker, Parker, Brody, & Schoenberg, 1982).

Constructing the Critical Life Events Survey. Adolescents are willing to discuss critical incidents—their own or those of others—when they feel comfortable about the context. They need reasonable assurance of confidentiality and a place where they will not have to make a public display of their misfortunes. But, perhaps more important, they need an organized format in which to present their experiences, which can be quite complex and confusing, and they need terminology available to them that is clear and unambiguous. For this reason a peer advisory group was formed of some 30 adolescents to help construct the questionnaire and determine language appropriate to it.

The group began by brainstorming the range of events that could befall children in the process of growing up and that would possibly be traumatic. Similar events were then consolidated, and extreme, fanciful, or wildly improbable events were eliminated from the list. The remaining items were rank ordered according to the group's perception of the severity of the event. Terminology was examined to ensure accessibility and clarity. Finally, 16 items were chosen as the most important. Several questions were formulated that could be answered with a yes or no, by using a Likert-type scale, or (in the case of age) directly with numerical answer. These questions were then placed on a grid format so the respondent could first indicate whether a specific critical life event had occurred and then answer the various questions concerning that event.

Constructing the Parental/Adult Response to Crisis Check-list. This same group of advisory peers was then asked to list, in their own words, all of the ways in which adults had responded to them when crises had occurred. Some 40 responses were recorded on a blackboard so that all could see. Each item was considered for clarity, and a number were revised, broken down into components, or eliminated because of generality or profanity. The group was asked to favor medium-generality terms (such as "listened well") rather than terms that were too general to be meaningful (such as "helped me") or too specific for the test situation (such as "maintained good eye contact"). The resulting list was rank ordered (from the worst to the best possible responses), and the top 10 and bottom 10 were selected. The resulting list of 20 parental responses was scrambled and listed in random order. Next to each response was a place to be checked if the response was experienced. Columns for mother, father, and other adult were provided. Respondents could then check just how those adults had responded to them during their worst crises.

Constructing the Current Maladaptive Adolescent Behavior Inventory. The literature is mixed about the validity of self-reports in areas of maladaptive behavior, tending to support their use but indicating that subjects have a tendency to underreport in cases of sexual abuse and overreport in cases of drug use. On the other hand, for the purposes of sampling the general population, self-reports are the best available, and, keeping the caveats in mind, can be considered generally reliable. In order to obtain the most reliable self-reports possible, the adolescent peer group was again involved to help construct a nonthreatening questionnaire.

Upon the group's advice, it was decided to allow respondents to evaluate their own maladaptive patterns in the sense of determining if their drug use was "heavy," for instance, or whether their suicidal ideation was "occasional" rather than "frequent." Further, it was determined upon their advice to keep the number of questions to a minimum. Likert-type scale responses were adopted to allow frequency data to reflect the extent of involvement in the particular behavior.

Constructing the Background and Current Status Questionnaire. Questions regarding parents' social/economic status and family structure were asked, as well as age and sex. With the exception of age, all responses required only checks in appropriate spaces.

PROCEDURES

The questionnaire packets were administered to subjects at their school classrooms by the experimenter and a group of four trained peer test administrators. The peers were trained during the pilot study and were available to answer questions, clarify terminology, and assist subjects in answering questionnaires when requested. The central function of the peer assistants was to circumvent possible fears of divulging sensitive material to adults. They were also trained to review questionnaires upon completion in a manner that did not disclose the content of the answers, in order to ensure as few missing answers and incomplete responses as possible. The questionnaires were administered to whole classes to minimize further the pressure to withhold information, and names were not asked in order to guarantee anonymity.

DATA ANALYSIS

Correlations between the variables were statistically determined; analyses of the hypotheses included intercorrelational matrices, factor analysis, and other analysis as appropriate. Each variable consisted of a set of items (e.g., MABs, the dependent variable, consisted of five items: drug and alcohol abuse, suicidal behaviors, and so on). The specific items as well as patterns of items were tested for correlation. Inferences were drawn from specific item relationships, according to the hypotheses.

LIMITATIONS

In order to assess the specific limitations of the study design, each possible source of invalidity as identified by Campbell and Stanley (1966) was explored and refuted (some of Campbell and Stanley's categories apply mainly to experimental or quasi-experimental designs and do not apply to this study).

Possible Threats to Internal Validity

Instrumentation. Aside from attendance at the continuation school (considered highly predictive of serious school attendance problems), the only instruments utilized in this study were the questionnaires. These remained constant across all groups being tested. One possible source of instrumentation invalidity was the procedure involving help in filling out portions of the questionnaire some students may have found confusing. The subject was able to choose either the tester or one of several student assistants to provide clarification. This was done to circumvent the inhibiting effects of either adult or peer or male or female interaction over sensitive information. The risk of contamination was controlled by the training of the assistants in how to clarify each question and how to project a warmly empathic but neutral position regarding content items. Missed responses were minimized by visual check by assistants, but subjects were first shown how to fold the questionnaire in such a way as to hide the content question from the assistant's view.

Another possible source of instrumentation invalidity concerns the reliability of the instrument itself. It was not known whether subjects would answer items concerning critical incidents the same way upon retest. This problem is compounded by the nature of the material being sampled. Obtaining a test-retest reliability coefficient would not be helpful in this case because of the contaminating reactive effects of testing. Pretest/posttest differences on retrospective self-reports regarding material of a highly sensitive nature are quite likely to differ, in that taking the test for the first time could well initiate a process of further recall within the subject. This has been termed the *preamble effect* by Cantril (1944) in his discussion of measurement as a change agent. At bottom, the issue of the adequacy of the instrument reduces to whether other methods (such as open-ended questions, personal interviews, or interviews with others) are likely to be better. It was determined that the value of anonymity as well as the structure and focus of the questionnaire offset the possible values of interviewer rapport or a more open-ended questionnaire. Further, interviewing others or researching records presented practical difficulties due to the sample size needed and would not reflect the subjects.

Differential Selection of Subjects. Because this design was constructed to sample background factors among differing groups, preexisting differences were controlled by stratification, not avoidance. In analyzing data, control groups for each background difference or each behavioral difference were formed from within the sample. Thus subjects in this study were used as their own controls. Taken to an extreme, groups of subjects could be selected according to the maladaptive behavior pattern they exhibited to ensure diversity. What makes that unattractive is the need to sample a wide range of adolescents and avoid the possible contaminating effects of statistical regression. Using conventional wisdom as a heuristic, then, it was determined that a representative sample of regular high school students (approximately 2/3 of the sample) combined with an adequate number of continuation students (approximately 1/3 of the sample, who ensured an adequate sampling of maladaptive behaviors) provided sufficient diversity and an approximation of representativeness. As the purpose of the sampling was to explore background differences in relation to current behavior (as opposed to determining relative frequencies of current behavior), this approximate representativeness was deemed to provide adequate protection against threats to internal validity due to selection bias.

As to the extent to which the sample adequately represents the population studied, it must be made clear that the sample is non-random but stratified, and generalizations are limited to the populations studied. Stratification measures include parameters to maximize representation. As English classes are required of all comprehensive high school students, all students funnel through them. This presented a unique opportunity to access a stratified sample. The ten or so courses offered varied according to level (advanced, regular, remedial), and classes were sampled proportionately. This provided a roughly representative sample (n = 133) of all students in the school. The continuation school student sample included all those present on the day of testing, a total of 70 students.

Possible Threats to External Validity

Interaction Effects of Selection Bias. The population sampled includes 15–18-year-old adolescents from a predominantly Anglo, fairly stable, suburban middle-class community in Southern California. The first question is, assuming the subjects sampled to be representative of that population, to what extent are the results generalizable to a larger population? It must be answered that populations differing in significant ways (in terms of ethnic and socioeconomic class, inner city or rural, and so on) are likely to produce different results. Specifically, mean values of frequency of both background incidents and current behaviors could differ significantly as could the nature of each. Less obvious but more important, cultural and ethnic variables influencing family patterns of response toward children's crises could be expected to influence postcrisis functioning differentially. Indeed, that differential effect is one hypothesis the study sets out to establish. Among different groups, specific parental responses could differ in both frequency and meaning. Consequently, results of the study must be considered only tentatively generalizable, particularly among the parent response variables. Further, among diverse populations, the results may be of more heuristic than descriptive usefulness.

Reactive Effects of Experimental Arrangements. Of the several possible methods of sampling the data, the format of anonymous questionnaire was adopted on the following basis. Information about critical events in childhood involves evoking unpleasant memories and associations. Often subjects are unwilling to disclose such sensitive information publicly, because of fears of stigma, embarrassment, and rejection. To talk about an event with another person somehow raises a new issue of the meaning of the event and the adequacy with which one dealt with it then and now. Further, descriptions of current behavior frequently amount to admissions of guilt (legal or moral) and raise fears of social or legal consequences as well as personal rejection by the interviewer. For these reasons, an anonymous questionnaire was chosen as most likely to elicit accurate information by minimizing reactions of nondisclosure to the social pressure of interviewers. Second, scaled responses as well as checklists were constructed to assist subjects in organizing and presenting their experiences. This was deemed necessary because of the inhibiting effects upon memory and expression of painful or embarrassing experiences. Finally, in order to minimize the reactive effects of perceived adult censure, both male and female peer assistants helped administer the questionnaire and were available to answer questions regarding item and procedural clarification. These experimental arrangements were adopted upon recommendation by a panel of peers who were asked to comment on how the research could be done in a nonthreatening manner. It was felt that the above arrangements maximized the likelihood of sampling accurate information and minimized the possibility of reactive effects contaminating the data.

On the basis of the above considerations, it was concluded that the study design remains sound, and the results generalizable within the limits discussed in the section above on the interaction effects of selection bias.

This study sought to investigate the relationship between psychologically traumatic events in childhood (childhood critical incidents) and subsequent maladaptive behavior in adolescence. This ambitious project could perhaps be best pursued with a large sampling representing diverse regional and ethnic populations and studied longitudinally. Unobtrusive observers could record all critical incidents befalling the population, assess the involved family and support system dynamics surrounding each child at the time of the incident, and follow each child into adolescence to assess his or her behavior further. Several difficulties are inherent in such an approach, however. First, it would take 15 to 18 years to complete the project. Second, a prohibitively large research team would be required. Third, and more important, observations and cross-validations do not capture what is essentially a highly personal and subjective event. Often traumas are aggravated by the responses of those surrounding the victim; consequently the interaction itself is suspect, as is the appraisal of the event by family or outside observers. Finally, any such presence of observers and testers would contaminate the situation with possible reactive effects.

Memory is notoriously subject to distortion, exaggeration, and selective amnesia. This makes the subject's recall of childhood events a tenuous data base from which to draw generalizations. However, due to the considerations noted above regarding outside observers, and due to the same vulnerability on the part of family or other involved persons, combined with the inherent subjectivity of trauma, the subjects themselves appeared to present the best possible source of information regarding their own critical incidents.

Thus this study approached the subjects themselves, specifically, a population of Southern California, predominantly Anglo, middle-class adolescents. These adolescents were queried as to their backgrounds, their history of critical incidents, the manner in which their parents or other significant adults responded to their crises, and their current behavior. Anonymous questionnaires were utilized for reasons outlined above and were developed with the assistance of a panel of some 30 adolescents in order to maximize accessibility and relevance.

RESULTS

This research study investigated the relationship between children's background of critical incidents and subsequent maladaptive behavior. Specifically, two questions were addressed:

1. Are childhood critical incidents associated with maladaptive adolescent behavior?

2. In what way do parents' manner of responding to their children's critical incidents affect subsequent maladaptive behavior during adolescence?

DESCRIPTION OF THE SAMPLE

This section consists of three parts. First, the various characteristics of the research sample will be described, including student demographics, family demographics, and students' past experiences and current behavior. Second, a description of the scale construction used in testing the hypotheses is offered. Construction of the critical incidents scale and maladaptive adolescent behaviors scale, as well as the parental response index, is described, and reliability of the scales reported. Third, the various relationships found among the data that bear upon the research questions will be presented.

Student Demographics. Students surveyed ranged in age from 15 to 19 years, with 17-year-olds constituting 46% of the sample. Table A.1 indicates frequencies and percentages of age groups represented. Subjects were nearly evenly distributed by sex: 105 were male (52%) and 98 were female (48%). A total of 75% were Anglo; the remaining 25% were divided nearly evenly among Blacks, Hispanics, and Asians.

The sample was compared on the basis of family composition, education, and occupation. In terms of composition, 56% reported living with both parents, 27% with a single parent, and 12% with a parent or stepparent.

Finally, the students were compared as to what sorts of maladaptive behaviors they had engaged in. Each of these was reported in the form of frequency, ranging from the extremes of "none" to "often" in appropriate terms.

Table A.1: Ages of the Students Participating in This Study

Age	Students from Regular School		Students from Continuation School	
	n	%	n	%
14	3	2.2	2	2.9
15	1	.8		
16	23	17.3	32	45.7
17	71	553.4	23	32.9
18	30	22.6	12	17.1
19	5	3.8	1	1.4
Total	133	100.0	70	100.0
$\overline{X}$	17.05		16.66	

SCALE CONSTRUCTION

Scales for each variable were constructed to allow analysis of data provided by the study in order to test the hypotheses. The construction of these scales is described below and reliability data provided.

Constructing the Critical Incidents Scale. A simple scale for critical incidents was constructed. This was summative, a simple count of the types of incidents experienced (not their quality or intensity). Table A.2 indicates the percentage of the sample experiencing each type of incident. The most frequently experienced event was the death of someone close, which was experienced by 57% of the sample. The mean frequency of events was 2.66, with 12% experiencing no incident on the list and 11% reporting 6 to (a maximum of) 10 events. The experiences of the sample are summarized in Table A.2.

Table A.2: Frequencies for Critical Incidents

	Students Experiencing Event	
Event	*n*	*%*
Death of parent	11	5
Death of someone close	115	57
Frequent moves	84	41
Physical-mental abuse	31	15
Sexual assault	16	08
Serious accident	33	16
Child molestation	6	3
Pressure by gangs	12	6
Foster placement	12	6
Mental hospital/group home	16	8
Parental rejection	28	1
Fail school by sixth grade	8	4
Divorce/stepparent conflict	69	34
Parent fighting	84	41
Alcoholism-family	39	19
Incest	1	

NOTE: The total sample size was 203. Of this number, 24 experienced none of the critical life events included in this study.

Constructing the Maladaptive Behaviors Scale. Two methods of constructing the maladaptive behaviors scale were considered. The first was a simple count of the behaviors engaged in by the students, each behavior weighted by the intensity of the experience. Students could engage in from 0 to 6 behaviors. Frequencies were as follows: 33% of the sample engaged in 0–1 behavior, while 30% engaged in 4 or more. When these frequencies are weighted by intensity of experience, reliability for the resulting scale (measured by Cronbach's alpha) was .75. This scale provided a numerical value which directly represented behaviors in the world for comparison purposes. In other words, groups of students could be compared using this scale without the confusion introduced by an elaborate weighting system. Cronbach's alpha for this scale is .75.

From a clinical perspective, however, this scale lacks sensitivity to the important differences between types of maladaptive behavior. There is a qualitative difference between an occasional beer and one attempt at suicide. In order to increase the variability of the scale by incorporating clinical judgments of the relative importance of the different behaviors, an attempt was made at devising a weighted scale. This weighting scheme ranked behaviors in terms of clinical seriousness or importance.

After consultation with two other judges, the following scheme was employed for the purposes of weighting. In cases of runaways, one time was added to frequency count if any of the times exceeded one night. The usage level of cocaine was computed at 1.5 times marijuana or alcohol. As suicide attempts were considered the most serious on the list, attempts were multiplied by two and an extra point was added for frequent thoughts. This attempt at weighting is arbitrary, but it appears to be an improvement over no weighting system at all.

Frequencies of maladaptive behaviors in the sample utilizing this weighted scale are presented in Table A.3. Cronbach's alpha for this scale remains .75, providing a reliable scale that reflects the relative seriousness of the behavior.

Constructing the Parental Response Index. Prior to the study, a group of 20 students was asked to generate a list of the ways parents might respond to their children's crises. The result-

TABLE A.3: Number of MABs Experienced by Students

Number of MABs	Students from Regular School		Students from Continuation School	
	n	*%*	*n*	*%*
0	49	39.8		
1	53	39.8	5	7.1
2	21	15.8	13	18.6
3	7	5.3	11	15.78
4	3	2.3	18	25.7
5			19	27.1
6			4	5.7

ing list of 35 responses was ranked from most to least helpful, as judged by the students. The best and worst responses were then randomized and incorporated into a checklist.

In the current study, students were asked to check off those responses that their parents actually adopted during their (the students') crises. Students indicated how their mothers responded to their crisis and how their fathers responded to their crisis. A principal components factor analysis was performed on each set of parent data to see whether particular parental responses coalesced into identifiable modes or styles of response. The factor loadings for mothers' and fathers' responses are given in Table A.4 and A.5 respectively. These tables present the correlations of particular responses with the factors (modes of response), as well as the reliability of the scales suggested by the factors. The mothers' modes of reacting to their children's crises are shown in Table A.4. On the basis of an informal content analysis of the factor loadings, factors were named for the apparent emotional set underlying them. Factor 1 consisted of items suggesting warmth, acceptance, and accessibility and is consequently named "supportive." Factor 2 consisted of items suggesting a focus upon the parent's own reactions rather than upon those of the child. Thus Factor 2 was named "withholding." Factor 3 consisted of items suggesting an inability to deal with the child or the situation in an effective manner and is named "incompetent." Cronbach's alpha for these scales is .88, .75, and .62 respectively. The relatively low reliability of scale 3 is

Table A.4: Mothers' Responses to Crisis

Variables	Factor Loadings: Three Factors		
	1	*2*	*3*
Expressed worry	.52		
Allowed me to talk	.66		
Showed warmth, acceptance	.69		
Gave reasonable assurance	.70		
Listened well	.67		
Respected privacy	.57		
Came through in past	.62		
Showed patience	.70		
Showed understanding	.68		
Made helpful suggestions	.67		
Was there when needed	.70		
Focused on self		.74	
Denied seriousness		.76	
Shrugged off my feelings		.64	
Concerned about how it affected self		.56	
Unable to cope			.71
Told me not to talk about it			.55
Made false assurances			.73
Eigenvalue	6.73	2.21	1.24
Percentage variance explained	34	11	6
Reliability Cronbach's alpha	.88	.75	.62

perhaps explained by the fact that the mothers' largely negative responses were split between Factors 2 and 3, leaving only three items in Factor 3. The resulting three styles of children's crisis management will be associated with adolescent behavioral outcomes in the next section.

The fathers' modes of reacting to their children's crises are shown in Table A.5. Two factors were derived from the fathers' responses and named in the same manner as those of the mothers. While content items in Factor 1 differed slightly, the apparent

Table A.5: Fathers' Response to Crisis

Variables	Factor Loadings: Two Factors	
	1	*2*
Was there when needed	.80	
Made helpful suggestions	.77	
Came through	.77	
Showed warmth	.74	
Showed understanding	.73	
Showed patience	.73	
Listened well	.71	
Gave reassurance	.70	
Allowed me to talk	.70	
Made assumptions		.71
Blamed me		.69
Shrugged off my feelings		.67
Concerned with self		.67
Focused on self		.67
Made false assurances		.58
Didn't want to talk		.56
Eigenvalue	6.70	2.87
Percentage variance explained	33.3	14.3
Reliability Cronbach's alpha	.91	.80

underlying emotional set appears to be clearly the same, so Factor 1 was also labeled "supportive." Factor 2 consisted of a content item reflecting an apparently mixed emotional set including elements of overreaction and escapism; thus it was termed "reactive/escapist." Cronbach's alpha for these scales is .91 and .79.

RELATIONSHIPS FOUND AMONG THE DATA

The scales described in the previous section were devised in order to test the hypotheses of the study. This section describes that testing and reports the extent to which the data support those hypotheses. Hypothesis 1 reads as follows:

Hypothesis 1. There will be a significant positive correlation between childhood critical incidents and the frequency of maladaptive adolescent behaviors as measured by self-reports (on the Critical Life Events Survey and Current Maladaptive Adolescent Behavior Inventory).

Thus this hypothesis concerned the relationship between the critical incidents scale and the maladaptive behaviors scale. To determine this relationship, two questions were asked. The first concerned whether the students who were engaging in maladaptive behaviors were the same students who had experienced many critical incidents.

To explore this relationship, the critical incidents summative scale was divided into a trichotomy, creating three groups of students roughly equal in number. The first group had experienced few critical incidents (0–1 events); this group constituted 33% of the sample. The second group, constituting 37% of the sample, had experienced a moderate number of critical incidents (2–3). The third group had experienced many events (4–10) and made up 30% of the sample.

These three groups were then compared as to whether they differed on their weighted maladaptive behaviors scale scores. A one-way analysis of variance was performed on the weighted maladaptive behaviors scale scores of the three groups. There was indeed a difference between groups, F, 189 = 25.87, p<.001.

The second question asked relative to Hypothesis 1 had to do with whether the relationship between childhood critical incidents and maladaptive adolescent behaviors was linear. That is, were MAB scale score levels related positively to CCI scale levels? To answer this question, a correlation analysis was conducted. Individual MAB items making up the composite scale were correlated with childhood critical incident scores. Individual correlation coefficients are reported in Table A.6.

On the basis of these results, it seems clear that adolescents' maladaptive behaviors are positively and significantly related to the number of critical events they have experienced.

Hypothesis 2. There will be a significant positive correlation between the freqency of negative parental/adult responses to chil-

**Table A.6: Correlation of Maladaptive Adolescent
Behaviors with Childhood Critical Incidents**

MAB	Correlation
Running away	r (202) = .37
Alcohol use	r (197) = .28
Marijuana use	r (196) = .35
Cocaine use	r (184) = .32
Suicide attempts	r (201) = .21
School attendance problems	r (203) = .39

dren's critical incidents and the frequency of the children's subsequent maladaptive adolescent behaviors as measured by self-
reports (on the Parental/Adult Response to Crisis Checklist and the
Current Maladaptive Adolescent Behavior Inventory).

This hypothesis concerns the relationships between the parental response scales and the maladaptive behaviors scale.

In investigating the manner in which parents responded to
their children's crises, we focused upon what the differences are
between parents' responses to crises for children who behave
maladaptively and for those who do not.

To explore this relationship, the maladaptive behaviors scale
was divided into a trichotomy. This created three groups of subjects
on the basis of the (weighted) frequency of their maladaptive behaviors:

1. few (0–1) maladaptive behaviors: 47% of the sample

2. moderate (2–3) maladaptive behaviors: 22% of the sample

3. many (4–6) maladaptive behaviors: 31% of the sample

The question asked was whether these groups differed in the
degree to which their parents' responses to crises could be characterized as being:

for mothers	*for fathers*
1. supportive	1. supportive
2. withholding	2. reactive/escapist
3. incompetent	

These response styles were derived from the factor analysis of the parent/adult responses as discussed above.

A one-way ANOVA, in which the between-groups factor was the level of maladaptive behavior experienced, was performed on the mothers' supportive response index to investigate this relationship. This analysis did not produce a group difference, indicating that mothers responding supportively did not significantly alter the outcome of the critical incident, at least in terms of maladaptive adolescent behaviors.

To investigate the possibility that students experiencing differing levels of maladaptive behavior differed in terms of their mothers' withholding responses, a one-way ANOVA was performed on the mothers' withholding index. This analysis revealed a strong group effect ($F[2, 185] = 6.5$, $p<.001$), with students in the high MAB group reporting more withholding responses among their mothers than those in the low MAB group.

Similar analyses were performed on the remaining three indices (mothers' inadequate index, fathers' supportive index, and fathers' reactive/escapist index). Strong group effects were found between students with high levels of maladaptive behaviors and both mothers' inadequate index ($F[2, 185] = 12.80$, $p<.001$) and fathers' reactive/escapist index ($F[2, 185] = 24.45$, $p<.001$). In addition, a significant effect was discovered between students with low levels of maladaptive behaviors and the fathers' supportive index ($F[2, 185] = 2.98$, $p<.05$). Students in the low MAB group reported a greater incidence of supportive responses from their fathers in reaction to crises than did students in the high MAB group.

The results of these analyses support the second hypothesis, namely, that parental response following children's critical incidents affects MABs. These findings indicate that mothers can have a significant negative effect by adopting withholding or inadequate response styles in the face of their children's critical incidents. Similarly, fathers can have a negative effect by adopting a reactive/escapist style. Fathers, however, can exert a positive effect by adopting a supportive style. However, no such positive effect was shown for mothers' supportive responses.

DISCUSSION

Data generated by the study supported both of the hypotheses. Hypothesis 1—that childhood critical incidents would correlate positively with subsequent maladaptive adolescent behaviors—was supported. This finding supports similar results of Harris's (1981) study of dropouts. It also amplifies those studies mentioned in the literature reviewed in Chapter II of this volume, of both specific CCIs and specific MABs. Literature concerning specific CCIs (e.g., Briere & Runtz, 1985; Klagsbrun & Davis, 1977; Priest, 1985) indicated that they could, separately, be considered antecedents to a range of subsequent MABs. Further, literature cited studying antecedents to specific MABs showed each of those behaviors to follow a range of antecedent CCIs (e.g., Anderson, 1981; Nilson, 1981; Robins et al., 1977). This study confirmed that a general relationship between CCIs and MABs exists.

Because so many confounding variables exist in determining the cause of maladaptive behavior, it would be unfounded to attribute causal agency to CCIs for subsequent MABs. However, there is no evidence to suggest that CCIs stand as necessary and sufficient conditions for MABs to occur. Indeed, part of this study concerned with assessing the effects of parents' responses to their children's crises indicated that various factors can mitigate the effects of CCIs. It can be safely stated, however, that CCIs are strongly contributing factors to the development of maladaptive adolescent behavior.

Hypothesis 2 was also supported, namely, that certain parental responses to children's crises are associated with subsequent maladaptive adolescent behavior; mothers' "withdrawal" and "incompetent" responses and fathers' "reactive/escapist" responses. Of considerable interest in this study is the definition of parental response styles that are predictive of outcomes in terms of MAB development. These will be summarized below. Those responses associated with positive outcomes for fathers (fathers' "supportive" index) are listed in the Results section (as are the rest of the profiles). Interestingly, the corresponding factor for mothers (mothers' "supportive" index), which consisted of responses nearly identical to those of fathers (differing slightly in ranking of items) did not correspond with positive (low MAB) outcome.

Mothers, it seems, cannot do anything right, at least according to adolescents.

Upon further reflection, it may be that this discrepancy indicates a cultural bias toward sex-role expectations. It stands to reason—due to culturally evolved expectations—that mothers are expected to be warm, supportive, and empathic, and that fathers are not; no one expects fathers to come through in a crisis, and everyone expects mothers to. Because of this bias, if a mother does not come through (withdraws or proves inadequate in terms of responsibilities), it is considered a serious breach; if she does come through, it is considered only as it should be. Similarly, if a father fails to respond with all of the positive virtues, it is par for the course, but if he manages to rise to the occasion, it is an event of some consequence. This somewhat cynical interpretation seems to make sense of an otherwise puzzling discrepancy. Further research on this issue might investigate children's role expectations regarding mothers' and fathers' behavior.

Similarly, while mothers seem to suffer by having two response profiles that result in compounding the effects of trauma, fathers have only one. This again makes a certain sense if one assumes that mothers are expected to be there emotionally for their children and men are not. Reversing the profiles for a moment, men might be expected to withdraw or be inadequate in terms of emotional response, but it is only when they initially overreact and then remove themselves emotionally that traumas are compounded. Mothers' initial overreactions may be expected, however.

The results of this study suggest several ways in which parents can respond positively to their children's crises and several responses they should avoid. In general, following a crisis parents should allow children to talk about the incident and its ramifications, showing patience and understanding and using listening techniques that convey to the child that they did, in fact, hear what was said. Parents can offer suggestions and assurances, but not to the extent that they are experienced as impositions or as denying the importance of the event or its attendant feelings.

It is important for fathers not to initially overreact and then avoid the situation. It is equally important for mothers not to withdraw emotionally from the event or become focused upon themselves, and it is important for them to maintain composure and not to "fall apart."

It is the contention of this author that the most useful explanatory construct available to make sense of the relationship between CCIs and MABs is that of Posttraumatic Stress Disorder. This construct is explored with particular emphasis upon the manner in which posttraumatic stress interacts with normal development and the evolution of symptomatology among children and adolescents in Chapter II of this volume. Chapter III elaborates on the implications of adult response styles for the child in crisis.

Background and Current Status Questionnaire (BARC)

1. Your age _____

2. Male _____   Female _____

3. What adults are you currently living with? Please check one:

    Both Parents   _____

    Single Parent   _____

    Parent plus Stepparent   _____

    Adoptive Parents   _____

    Relatives   _____

    Other   _____

4. What is the highest level of EDUCATION attained by the adults you are living with? Please check one:

	(step-) MOTHER	(step-) FATHER
Completed High School	_____	_____
Attended College	_____	_____
College Graduate	_____	_____
Below High School	_____	_____

5. What are their OCCUPATIONS? Please check one:

	(step-) MOTHER	(step-) FATHER
Professional/Technical	_____	_____
Manager/Business Person	_____	_____
Clerical/Sales/Secretary	_____	_____
Craftsman/Foreman	_____	_____
Laborer	_____	_____
Other	_____	_____

6. Your ETHNIC Group?

    White ___   Black ___   Asian ___   Hispanic ___   Other ___

Current Maladaptive Adolescent Behavior Inventory (CMABI)

1. Some students have *run away* from home. How often have you?

   Never ____   Once ____   2–3 Times ____   More Than 3 ____

   How long at a time?

   1 Night ____   2–3 Nights ____   Longer ____

2. *Alcohol* and/or *Drugs:* If alcohol or drug use is something you have experienced, please check appropriate squares below to indicate usage:

	Never	Tried Once	Several Times	Occasional Use	Frequent Use	Heavy Use
Alcohol	[ ]	[ ]	[ ]	[ ]	[ ]	[ ]
Pot	[ ]	[ ]	[ ]	[ ]	[ ]	[ ]
Cocaine	[ ]	[ ]	[ ]	[ ]	[ ]	[ ]
Other	[ ]	[ ]	[ ]	[ ]	[ ]	[ ]

3. At some time in their lives some people have wished they could just go to sleep and never wake up. Some people think about actually killing themselves.

   Have you wished you were dead?

   Never ____   Once or Twice ____   Occasionally ____   Frequently ____

   Have you thought about killing yourself?

   Never ____   Once or Twice ____   Occasionally ____   Frequently ____

   Have you ever tried?

   Never ____   Once ____   More than once ____

4. For Women Only:

   Have you ever been pregnant? Yes ____ No ____

   How many times?

   Once ____ Twice ____ Three or more times ____

The next page asks you to list *Critical Life Events* you have experienced. Those are events so powerful that coping is difficult. At the end of the page you will have a chance to list repeat events or those not listed.

Take your time, and ask questions if you get confused. You will find that it really will be easier and faster than it first appears.

Thanks!!

Critical Life Event

Directions: If any of the following events happened to you, check YES, the rest of the questions. THANKS!

	Did the event happen to you?	*How old were you at the time?*	*How much did it affect you?* *1–just a little* *2–a little more* *3–a lot* *4–very seriously* *5–devastating*
EVENT	*circle*	*write in*	*circle*
1. Death of a parent	Y / N	( )	1 2 3 4 5
2. Death of someone close	Y / N	( )	1 2 3 4 5
3. Frequent moves/ school changes	Y / N	( )	1 2 3 4 5
4. Physical or mental abuse	Y / N	( )	1 2 3 4 5
5. Sexual assault/rape	Y / N	( )	1 2 3 4 5
6. Serious accident or natural disaster	Y / N	( )	1 2 3 4 5
7. Child molestation	Y / N	( )	1 2 3 4 5
8. Pressure by gangs	Y / N	( )	1 2 3 4 5
9. Foster placement or abandonment	Y / N	( )	1 2 3 4 5
10. Commitment to mental hospital or group home	Y / N	( )	1 2 3 4 5
11. Rejection by parents	Y / N	( )	1 2 3 4 5
12. School failure by 6th grade	Y / N	( )	1 2 3 4 5
13. Divorce and/or stepparent conflict	Y / N	( )	1 2 3 4 5
14. Parental fighting	Y / N	( )	1 2 3 4 5
15. Alcoholism in the family	Y / N	( )	1 2 3 4 5
16. Incest	Y / N	( )	1 2 3 4 5
Were any of these events repeated?			
17. (fill in)	Y / N	( )	1 2 3 4 5
18.	Y / N	( )	1 2 3 4 5
Any other really bad things not listed above?			
19.	Y / N	( )	1 2 3 4 5
20.	Y / N	( )	1 2 3 4 5

Survey (CLES) (Confidential)

note your age when it happened, and CIRCLE the appropriate number on

How did your Mom respond to you at the time? 1–not supportive 2–just a little 3–so-so 4–fairly supportive 5–very supportive	*How did your Dad respond to you at the time?* (use same answering system as for Mom)	*What about adults (such as relatives or teachers)?*	*How stable was your family at the time?* 1–very unstable/ insecure 2–unstable/ insecure 3–so-so 4–fairly stable/ secure 5–very stable/ secure
circle	*circle*	*circle*	*circle*
1 2 3 4 5	1 2 3 4 5	1 2 3 4 5	1 2 3 4 5
1 2 3 4 5	1 2 3 4 5	1 2 3 4 5	1 2 3 4 5
1 2 3 4 5	1 2 3 4 5	1 2 3 4 5	1 2 3 4 5
1 2 3 4 5	1 2 3 4 5	1 2 3 4 5	1 2 3 4 5
1 2 3 4 5	1 2 3 4 5	1 2 3 4 5	1 2 3 4 5
1 2 3 4 5	1 2 3 4 5	1 2 3 4 5	1 2 3 4 5
1 2 3 4 5	1 2 3 4 5	1 2 3 4 5	1 2 3 4 5
1 2 3 4 5	1 2 3 4 5	1 2 3 4 5	1 2 3 4 5
1 2 3 4 5	1 2 3 4 5	1 2 3 4 5	1 2 3 4 5
1 2 3 4 5	1 2 3 4 5	1 2 3 4 5	1 2 3 4 5
1 2 3 4 5	1 2 3 4 5	1 2 3 4 5	1 2 3 4 5
1 2 3 4 5	1 2 3 4 5	1 2 3 4 5	1 2 3 4 5
1 2 3 4 5	1 2 3 4 5	1 2 3 4 5	1 2 3 4 5
1 2 3 4 5	1 2 3 4 5	1 2 3 4 5	1 2 3 4 5
1 2 3 4 5	1 2 3 4 5	1 2 3 4 5	1 2 3 4 5
1 2 3 4 5	1 2 3 4 5	1 2 3 4 5	1 2 3 4 5

If so, fill in the one or two most important, and answer as before

1 2 3 4 5	1 2 3 4 5	1 2 3 4 5	1 2 3 4 5
1 2 3 4 5	1 2 3 4 5	1 2 3 4 5	1 2 3 4 5

If so, fill in the one or two most important below

1 2 3 4 5	1 2 3 4 5	1 2 3 4 5	1 2 3 4 5
1 2 3 4 5	1 2 3 4 5	1 2 3 4 5	1 2 3 4 5

Parental/Adult Response to Crisis Checklist (PARC)

On this page you are asked to describe how parents or other significant adults responded to you during your crisis, or during the weeks or months afterwards.

Place a *Check* after the things they *Did* do for the most part. Leave the things they did not do *Blank*. (If they did different things in different situations, check what they did after the most *Serious* incident.)

	Mother	Father	Other Important Adults
ADULT RESPONSE			
1. Expressed worry	___	___	___
2. They were unable to cope (couldn't meet responsibilities)	___	___	___
3. Made assumptions or jumped to conclusions too quickly	___	___	___
4. Allowed me to talk	___	___	___
5. Showed warmth, acceptance	___	___	___
6. Focused on themselves, not me	___	___	___
7. Denied the seriousness of the incident	___	___	___
8. Shrugged off my feelings	___	___	___
9. Gave reasonable reassurance	___	___	___
10. Listened well	___	___	___
11. They respected my privacy	___	___	___
12. Concerned about what it meant to them, not me	___	___	___
13. Told me not to talk about it (Don't be a crybaby)	___	___	___
14. They had come through for me in the past	___	___	___
15. They made false assurances (unrealistic promises)	___	___	___
16. They showed more patience	___	___	___
17. They blamed me	___	___	___
18. Let me know they understood by what they did and said	___	___	___
19. Made helpful suggestions, but didn't push	___	___	___
20. Reliability: They were there when I needed them	___	___	___

APPENDIX II

RESOURCES

A LARGE NUMBER of local public agencies and organizations provide information and services relating to children in crisis. This appendix lists possible starting points for those seeking help in this area, starting with the following institutions or agencies that are close at hand.

1. *Schools and school districts* frequently have extensive resources that are not widely known. Start with school psychologists and resource specialists, and explore for hidden human and material resources at home first.

2. *County and state departments of education, mental health, and social services* frequently provide free or low-cost services, including consultation. Consultants from these agencies are usually well trained and willing to assist through individual conferencing, staff training, or networking local talent. Often one person will specialize in crisis-related services, and that fact will be known to others in the office. A phone call to anyone in that office is usually the best way to get in touch with the right person.

3. *Private mental health agencies* are often good resources, as are special groups such as Parents United, Alcoholics Anonymous, Narcotics Anonymous, and others. Private agencies will often provide free or inexpensive consultation in exchange for community goodwill. Ask others on your staff for referral. Also, be clear with them that your understanding is that the service is gratis, and that they do not expect to be paid.

In addition, a number of private national organizations offer literature, materials, and services that can be of great assistance. Many of the most helpful are listed below:

Action for Child Protection, 428 4th Street, Suite 5, Annapolis, MD 21403 *(202)393-1090*

American Academy of Pediatrics, 141 Northwest Point Boulevard, Elk Grove Village, IL 60007 (800)433-9016 or (312) 228-5005

American Bar Association, National Legal Resource Center for Child Advocacy and Protection, 1800 M Street, N.W., Suite 200, South Lobby, Washington, DC 20036 (202)331-2250

American Civil Liberties Union, Children's Rights Project, 132 West 43rd Street, New York, NY 10036 (212)944-9800

American Humane Association, American Association for Protecting Children, 9725 East Hampden Avenue, Denver, CO 80231 (303)695-0811

American Medical Association, Health and Human Behavior Department, 535 North Dearborn Street, Chicago, IL 60610 (312)645-4523

American Psychological Association, 1200 17th Street, N.W., Washington, DC 20036 (202)955-7600

American Public Welfare Association, 1125 15th Street, N.W., Suite 300, Washington, DC 20005 (202)293-7550

Association of American Indian Affairs, Inc., 95 Madison Avenue, Suite 1407, New York, NY 10016 (212)689-8720

Big Brothers/Big Sisters of America, 230 North 13th Street, Philadelphia, PA 19107 (215)567-7000

Boys Club of America, Government Relations Office, 611 Rockville Pike, Suite 230, Rockville, MD 20852 (301)251-6676

C. Henry Kempe Center for Prevention and Treatment of

Child Abuse and Neglect, 1205 Oneida Street, Denver, CO 80220 (303)321-3963

Child Find, Inc., P.O. Box 277, New Paltz, NY 12561 (914)255- 1848

Child Welfare League of America, 440 First Street, N.W., Suite 310, Washington, DC 20001 (202)638-2952

Families Anonymous, Inc., P.O. Box 528, Van Nuys, CA 91408 (818)989-7841

Family Services America, 11700 West Lake Park Drive, Park Place, Milwaukee, WI 53224 (414)359-2111

Institute For The Community As Extended Family (ICEF), P.O. Box 952, San Jose, CA 95108 (408)280-5055

Missing Children Hotline, 300 Orchard City Drive, Suite 151, Campbell, CA 95008 (800)235-3535

National Association of Black Social Workers, 642 Beckwith Court, S.W., Atlanta, GA 30314 (404)584-7967

National Association of Social Workers, 7981 Eastern Avenue, Silver Spring, MD 20910 (301)565-0333

National Black Child Development Institute, 1463 Rhode Island Avenue, N.W., Washington, DC 20005 (202)387-1281

National Center For Child Abuse And Neglect (NCCAN); Children's Bureau Administration For Children, Youth And Families; Office Of Human Development Services; Department Of Health And Human Services, P.O. Box 1182, Washington, DC 20013 (202)245-2859

National Center for Missing and Exploited Children; Education, Prevention and Public Awareness Division, 1835 K

Street, N.W., Suite 600, Washington, DC 20006 (202)634-9821 or (800)843-5678

National Council of Jewish Women, Children and Youth Priority, Program Department, 53 West 23rd Street, New York, NY 10010 (212)645-4048

National Council of Juvenile and Family Court Judges, P.O. Box 8970, Reno, NV 89507 (702)784-6012

National Council on Child Abuse and Family Violence, 1155 Connecticut Avenue, N.W., Suite 300, Wash- ington, DC 20036 (800)222-2000 or (202)429-6695

National Crime Prevention Council, 733 15th Street, N.W., Suite 540, Washington, DC 20005 (202)393-7141

National Education Association, Human and Civil Rights Unit, 1201 16th Street, N.W., Washington DC 20036 (202)822-7711

National Exchange Club Foundation for Prevention of Child Abuse, 3050 Central Avenue, Toledo, OH 43606 (419)535-3232

National Child Abuse Hotline: Childhelp, U.S.A., P.O. Box 630, Hollywood, CA 90028 (800)4-A-CHILD

National Committee for the Prevention of Child Abuse (NCPCA), 332 South Michigan Avenue, Suite 950, Chicago, IL 60604 (312)663- 3520

Parents Anonymous, 6733 South Sepulveda, Suite 270, Los Angeles, CA 90045 (800)352-0386 (in California), (800)421-0353 (all other states) or (213)410-9732 (office)

Parents United/Daughters and Sons United/Adults Molested as Children United, P.O. Box 952, San Jose, CA 95108

(408)280-5055

Save the Children, National Office, 54 Wilton Road, Westport, CT 06880 (203)226-7271

National Network of Runaway and Youth Services, 1400 I Street, N.W., Suite 330, Washington, DC 20005 (202)682-4114

National Runaway Hotline, (800)231-6946

National Runaway Switchboard, (800)621-4000

SCAN (Stop Child Abuse and Neglect) Associates, P.O. Box 7445, Little Rock, AR 72217 (501)661-1474

Volunteers of America, 340 West 85th Street, New York, NY 10024 (212)873-2600

BIBLIOGRAPHY

Abbott, M. W., & Gregson, A. M. (1981). Cognitive dysfunction in the predication of relapse in alcoholics. *Journal of Studies in Alcoholics, 41*(3), 230–243.

Abelson, H. I., Fishburn, P. M., & Cisin, I. (1977). *National survey on drug abuse.* Washington, DC: National Institute on Drug Abuse, U.S. Department of Health, Education and Welfare.

Aguilera, D. C., and Messick, J. M. (1982). *Crisis intervention: Therapy for psychological emergencies.* St. Louis: C. V. Mosby.

Alline, V. (1947). *Play therapy.* New York: Ballantine.

American Psychiatric Association. (1980). *Diagnostic and statistical manual* (3rd ed.). Washington, DC: Author

American Psychiatric Association. (1987). *Diagnostic and statistical manual* (3rd ed., rev.). Washington, DC: Author

Anderson, D. (1981). Self-destructive behavior in children and adolescents. In C. F. Wells & I. R. Stuart (Eds.), *Self-destructive behavior in children and adolescents.* New York: Van Nostrand Reinhold.

Arroyo, W., & Eth, S. (1985). Children traumatized by Central American warfare. In S. Eth & R. S. Pynoos (Eds.), *Post-traumatic stress disorder in children.* Washington, DC: American Psychiatric Press.

Bard, M., & Sangrey, D. (1979). *The crime victim's book.* New York: Basic Books.

Barnes, G. E. (1979). Solvent abuse: A review. *International*

Journal of the Addictions, 14, 1–26.

Benedek, E. (1985). Children and psychic trauma: A brief review of contemporary thinking. In S. Eth & R. S. Pynoos (Eds.), *Post-traumatic stress disorder in children.* Washington, DC: American Psychiatric Press.

Birchnell, J. (1969). The possible consequence of early parental death. *British Journal of Medical Psychiatry, 42,* 1–12.

Black, C. (1979). Children of alcoholics. *Alcohol Health and Research World, 4,* 23–27.

Bloom, B. L., Asher, S. J., & White, S. W. (1978). Marital disruption as a stressor. *Psychological Bulletin, 85,* 867–894.

Bowen, M. (1978). *Family therapy in clinical practice.* New York: Jason Aronson.

Bowlby, J. (1961). The Adolf Meyer Lecture: Childhood mourning and its implications for psychiatry. *American Journal of Psychiatry, 118,* 481–498.

Bowlby, J. (1973). *Attachment and loss: Separation, anxiety and anger.* New York: Basic Books.

Brenner, T., Huizinga, D., & Elliott, D. S. (1978). *The social psychology of runaways.* Lexington, MA: Lexington Books.

Briere, J. (1984). *The effects of childhood sexual abuse on later psychological functioning: Defining a post-sexual-abuse syndrome.* Paper presented at the Third National Conference on Sexual Victimization of Children, Washington, DC.

Briere, J., & Runtz, M. (1985). *Symptomatology associated with prior sexual abuse in a non-clinical sample.* Paper presented at the annual meeting of the American Psychological Association, Los Angeles.

Briere, J., Runtz, M., & Lightfoot, A. (1978). *Suicidality in former sexual abuse victims*. Paper presented at the meetings of the American Association of Suicidology, Toronto.

Burgess, A., & Holstrom, L. (1974). Rape trauma syndrome. *American Journal of Psychiatry, 131*, 981–986.

Campbell, D. T., & Stanley, J. C. (1966). *Experimental and quasi-experimental designs for research*. Chicago: Rand McNally.

Cantril, H. (1944). *Gauging public opinion*. Princeton, NJ: Princeton University Press.

Chafetz, M. E., Blane, H. T., & Hill, M. J. (1971). Children of alcoholics: Observations in a child guidance clinic. *Quarterly Journal of Alcohol, 32*, 687–689.

Coleman, F. W., & Coleman, W. S. (1984). Helping siblings and other peers cope with dying. In H. Wass & C. A. Corr (Eds.), *Childhood and death*. Washington, DC: Hemisphere.

Coleman, J. C., Butcher, J. N., & Carson, R. L. (1980). *Abnormal psychology and modern life*. Glenville, IL: Scott Foresman.

Courtois, C. A. (1979). Characteristics of a volunteer sample of adult women who experienced incest in childhood or adolescence. *Dissertation Abstracts International, 40*, 2194A–3195A.

Donaldson, M. A., & Gardner, R. (1985). Diagnosis and treatment of traumatic stress among women after childhood incest. In C. R. Figley (Ed.), *Trauma and its wake*. New York: Brunner/Mazel.

Earle, E. (1979). The psychological effects of mutilating surgery in children and adolescents. *Psychoanalytic Study of the Child, 34*, 527–546.

Elkind, D. (1981). *The hurried child: Growing up too fast, too soon*. Reading, MA: Addison-Wesley.

Erickson, E. (1950). *Identity and the life cycle.* New York: International Universities Press.

Erickson, E. (1968). *Identity, youth and crisis.* New York: Norton.

Eth, S., & Pynoos, R. S. (1985a). Developmental perspective on psychic trauma in childhood. In C. R. Figley (Ed.), *Trauma and its wake.* New York: Brunner/Mazel.

Eth, S., & Pynoos, R. S. (Eds.). (1985b). *Post-traumatic stress disorder in children.* Washington, DC: American Psychiatric Press.

Eth, S., & Pynoos, R. S. (1985c). Children traumatized by witnessing acts of personal violence: Homicide, rape, or suicide behavior. In S. Eth & R. S. Pynoos (Eds.), *Post-traumatic stress disorder in children.* Washington, DC: American Psychiatric Press.

Eth, S., & Pynoos, R. S. (1985d). Interaction of trauma and grief in childhood. In S. Eth & R. S. Pynoos (Eds.), *Post-traumatic stress disorder in children.* Washington, DC: American Psychiatric Press.

Eth, S., Randolf, E., & Brown, J. (1988). Post-traumatic stress disorder. In J. Howell (Ed.), *Modern perspectives in the psychiatry of the neuroses.* New York: Brunner/Mazel.

Figley, C. R. (1985). From victim to survivor: Social responsibility in the wake of catastrophe. In C. R. Figley (Ed.), *Trauma and its wake.* New York: Brunner/Mazel.

Fine, E., Yudin, L. W., Holmes, J., & Hinemann, S. (1975, April). *Behavioral disorders in children with parental alcoholism.* Paper presented at the annual meeting of the National Council on Alcoholism, Milwaukee, WI.

Frears, L. H., & Schneider, J. M. (1981). Exploring loss and grief within a holistic framework. *Personnel and Guidance Journal, 59*(2), 341–345.

Fredrick, C. J. (1985a). An introduction and overview of youth suicide. In M. Peck, N. Farberow, & R. Litman (Eds.), *Youth suicide.* New York: Springer.

Fredrick, C. J. (1985b). Children traumatized by catastrophic situations. In S. Eth & R. S. Pynoos (Eds.), *Post-traumatic stress disorder in children.* Washington, DC: American Psychiatric Press.

Freud, S. (1920). Beyond the pleasure principle. In J. Strachey (Ed.), *The standard edition of the complete psychological works of Sigmund Freud* (Vol. 18). London: Hogarth.

Freud, S. (1926). Inhibitions, symptoms and anxiety. In J. Strachey (Ed.), *The standard edition of the complete psychological works of Sigmund Freud* (Vol. 18). London: Hogarth.

Freud, S. (1939). Moses and monotheism. In J. Strachey (Ed.), *The standard edition of the complete psychological works of Sigmund Freud* (Vol. 23). London: Hogarth.

Furman, E. (1984). Children's patterns in mourning the death of a loved one. In H. Wass and C. A. Corr (Eds.), *Childhood and death.* Washington, DC: Hemisphere.

Garmezy, N., & Rutter, M. (Eds.). (1983). *Stress, coping, and development in children.* New York: McGraw-Hill.

Gelles, R. (1978). Methods for studying sensitive family topics. *American Journal of Orthopsychiatry, 48,* 408–424.

Golan, N. (1981). *Passing through transitions.* New York: Free Press.

Green, A. (1985). Post-traumatic symptoms of incest victims.

In S. Eth & R. S. Pynoos (Eds.), *Post-traumatic stress disorder in children*. Washington, DC: American Psychiatric Press.

Gregory, I. (1965). Ante-retrospective data concerning childhood loss of a parent: Delinquents and high school drop-outs. *Archives of General Psychiatry, 13*, 99–109.

Gumser, R. J., Myrich, R., & Holdin, W.(1971). A study of play process in counseling. *Elementary School Guidance and Counseling, 5*, 256–263.

Harris, L. J. H. (1980). *Middle-class high school drop-outs: Incidents of physical abuse, incest, sexual assault, loss, symptomatic behaviors, and emotional disturbance*. Unpublished doctoral dissertation, University of Minnesota.

Havinghurst, R. J. (1972). *Developmental tasks and education*. New York: McKay.

Headington, B. J. (1981). Understanding a core experience: Loss. *Personnel and Guidance Journal, 59*(2), 338–341.

Heatherington, E. M., Cox, M., & Cox, R. (1978). *Family interaction and the social and cognitive development of children following divorce*. Washington, DC: Institute of Pediatric Service.

Hendlin, H. (1985). Suicide among the young: Psychodynamics and demography. In M. Peck, N. Farberow, & R. Litman (Eds.), *Youth suicide*. New York: Springer.

Herman, J. (1981). *Father-daughter incest*. Cambridge, MA: Harvard University Press.

Hindemann, M. (1976). Children of alcoholic parents. *Alcohol Health and Research World, 1*, 2–6.

Horowitz, M. (1976). *Stress response syndrome*. New York: Jason Aronson.

Horowitz, M. J., & Solomon, G. F. (1975). Delayed stress response syndrome in Vietnam veterans. *Journal of Social Issues, 31*, 67–80.

Horowitz, M. J., & Solomon, G. F. (1978). Delayed stress response in Vietnam veterans. In G. F. Figley (Ed.), *Stress disorders among Vietnam veterans.* New York: Brunner/Mazel.

Isaac, S. (1971). *Handbook in research and evaluation.* San Diego: Edits.

Jaremko, M. (1983). Stress inoculation training for social anxiety. In D. Meichelbaum & M. Jaremko (Eds.), *Stress reduction and prevention.* New York: Plenum.

Johnson, K. (1985). Family sculpture in the interpersonal relations classroom. *Journal of Continuation Education, 7,* 7–11.

Johnson, K. (1987). *Classroom crisis: A readi-reference guide.* Claremont, CA: Turnpoint.

Justice, B., & Duncan, D. F. (1976). Running away: An epidemic problem of adolescence. *Adolescence, 1,* 365–371.

Kaplan, H. S. (1979). *Disorders of sexual desire and other new concepts and techniques in sex therapy.* New York: Brunner/Mazel.

Khan, M. M. R. (1963). The concept of cumulative trauma. *Psychoanalytic Study of the Child, 18,* 286–306.

Klagsbrun, F., & Davis, D. E. (1977). Substance abuse and family interaction. *Family Process, 16,* 149–163.

Kramer, E. (1971). *Art as therapy with children.* New York: Schocken.

Kübler-Ross, E. (1969). *On death and dying.* New York: Macmillan.

Langer, T. S., & Michael, S. T. (1963). *Life stress and mental health.* New York: Free Press.

Lerner, M. (1970). The desire for justice and reactions to victims: Social psychological studies of some antecedents and consequences. In J. Macauley & L. Berkowitz (Eds.), *Altruism and helping behavior.* New York: Academic Press.

Lichter, S. O., Rapien, E. B., Seibert, F. M., & Sklansky, M. A. (1962). *The drop-outs: A treatment study of intellectually capable students who drop out of high school.* New York: Free Press.

Lidz, T., Fleck, S., & Cornelison, A. R. (1965). *Schizophrenia and the family.* New York: International University Press.

Lifton, R. (1979). *The broken connection.* New York: Simon & Schuster.

Lindemann, E. (1944). Symptomatology and management of acute grief. *American Journal of Psychiatry, 101,* 141–146.

Litman, R. E. (1976). Beyond crisis intervention. In E. Schneidman (Ed.), *Suicide: Contemporary developments.* New York: Grune & Stratton.

Lourie, I. S. (1977). The phenomenon of the abused adolescent: A clinical study. *Victimology, 2,* 268–276.

Lowenthal, M. F., & Chiriboga, D. (1973). Social stress and adaptation: Toward a life-course perspective. In C. Eisdorfer & M. P. Lawton (Eds.), *The psychology of adult development and aging.* Washington, DC: American Psychological Association.

Lustig, N., & Zeitlin, M. (1985). Bipolar affective disorder: A delinquent variable. In M. Peck, N. Farberow, and R. Litman

(Eds.), *Youth suicide*. New York: Springer.

Meichenbaum, D. (1983). *Stress inoculation training*. New York: Plenum.

Meizelman, K. (1978). *Incest: A psychological study of causes and effects with treatment recommendations*. San Francisco: Jossey-Bass.

Millman, R. B., Khuri, E. T., & Hammond, D. (1981). Perspectives on drug use and abuse. In C. F. Wells & I. R. Stuart (Eds.), *Self- destructive behavior in children and adolescents*. New York: Van Nostrand Reinhold.

Mitchell, J. (1983). When disaster strikes: The critical incident stress debriefing process. *Journal of Emergency Medical Services, 8,* 36–39.

Murphy, L., & Moriety, A. (1976). *Vulnerability, coping, and growth*. New Haven, CT: Yale University Press.

Myrich, R., & Holdin, W. (1971). A study of play process in counseling. *Elementary School Guidance and Counseling, 5,* 256–263.

Neidengard, T., & Yaliscove, D. (1981). Juvenile alcoholism and alcohol abuse. In C. F. Wells & I. R. Stuart (Eds.), *Self-destructive behavior in children and adolescents*. New York: Van Nostrand Reinhold.

Newman, C.J. (1976). Children of disaster: Clinical observations at Buffalo Creek. *American Journal of Psychiatry, 133,* 306–312.

Nilson, P. (1981). Psychological profiles of runaway children and adolescents. In C. F. Wells & I. R. Stuart (Eds.), *Self-destructive behavior in children and adolescents*. New York: Van Nostrand Reinhold.

Nir, Y. (1985). Post-traumatic stress disorder in children with cancer. In S. Eth & R. S. Pynoos (Eds.), *Post-traumatic stress disorder in children*. Washington, DC: American Psychiatric Press.

Norem-Hebeison, A., & Hedin, D. (1981). Influences on adolescent problem behavior. In U.S. Department of Health Services (Ed.), *Adolescent peer pressure*. Washington, DC: U.S. Department of Health Services.

Parker, E., Parker, D., Brody, J., & Schoenberg, R. (1982). Cognitive patterns of premature aging in male social drinkers. *Alcoholism: Clinical & Experimental Research, 6*(1), 46–52.

Peck, M. (1984). Youth suicide. In H. Wass & C. A. Corr (Eds.), *Childhood and death*. Washington, DC: Hemisphere.

Pfeffer, C. R. (1984). Death preoccupations and suicidal behavior in children. In H. Wass & C. A. Corr (Eds.), *Childhood and death*. Washington, DC: Hemisphere.

Pynoos, R. S., & Eth, S. (1984). Child as witness to homicide. *Journal of Social Issues, 40,* 87–108.

Richman, J. (1981). Family treatment of suicidal children and adolescents. In C. F. Wells and I. R. Stuart (Eds.), *Self-destructive behavior in children and adolescents*. New York: Van Nostrand Reinhold.

Robins, L. N., Davis, D. H., & Wish, E. (1977). Detecting predictors of rare events. In J. S. Strauss et al. (Eds.), *The origins and course of psychopathology*. New York: Plenum.

Rudd, L. (1981). Pregnancies and abortions. In C. F. Wells & I. R. Stuart (Eds.) *Self-destructive behavior in children and adolescents*. New York: Van Nostrand Reinhold.

Russell, D. H. (1981). On running away. In C. F. Wells & I. R. Stuart (Eds.), *Self-destructive behavior in children and adoles-*

cents. New York: Van Nostrand Reinhold.

Saarni, C., & Azara, V. (1981). Anxiety (developmental). In R. Woody (Ed.), *Encyclopedia of clinical assessment* (Vol. 2). San Francisco: Jossey-Bass.

Satir, V. (1967). *Conjoint family therapy*. Palo Alto, CA: Science and Behavior Books.

Schukit, M. A., Morrissey, E. R., Lewis, N. J., & Buck, W. T. (1977). Adolescent problem drinkers. In F. A. Seixus (Ed.), *Currents in alcoholism* (Vol. 2). New York: Grune & Stratton.

Scroi, S. M. (Ed.). (1976). *Handbook of clinical intervention in child sexual abuse*. Lexington, MA: Lexington Books.

Scurfield, R. M. (1985). Post-traumatic stress assessment and treatment: Overview and formulations. In C. R. Figley (Ed.), *Trauma and its wake*. New York: Brunner/Mazel.

Seligman, M. E., & Garber, J. (1980). *Human helplessness*. New York: Academic Press.

Shaffer, D., & Fisher, P. (1981). Suicide in children and young adolescents. In C. F. Wells & I. R. Stuart (Eds.), *Self-destructive behavior in children and adolescents*. New York: Van Nostrand Reinhold.

Siegler, M., Osmond, H., & Newell, S. (1968). Models of alcoholism. *Quarterly Journal of Studies of Alcoholism, 29*, 571–597.

Symonds, M. (1976). The rape victim: Psychological patterns of response. *American Journal of Psychoanalysis, 5*(1), 27–34.

Teicher, J. D. (1979). Suicide and suicide attempts. In J. D. Hoshpitz (Ed.), *Basic handbook of child psychiatry* (Vol. 2). New York: Basic Books.

Terr, L. C. (1979). The children of Chowchilla: A study of psychic trauma. *Psychoanalytic Study of the Child, 34,* 547–623.

Terr, L. C. (1981). Psychic trauma in children. *American Journal of Psychiatry, 138,* 14–19.

Terr, L. C. (1985). Children traumatized in small groups. In S. Eth & R. S. Pynoos (Eds.), *Post-traumatic stress disorder in children.* Washington, DC: American Psychiatric Press.

Thorneburg, H. D. (1975). Attitudinal determinants in holding dropouts in school. *Journal of Education Research, 68,* 181–185.

Trimble, M. R. (1981). *Post-traumatic neurosis.* Chichester: John Wiley.

Trimble, M. R. (1985). Post-traumatic stress disorder: History of a concept. In C. R. Figley (Ed.), *Trauma and its wake.* New York: Brunner/Mazel.

Tsai, M., Feldman-Summers, S., & Edgar, M. (1979). Child molestation: Variables related to differential impacts on psychosexual functioning in adult women. *Journal of Abnormal Psychology, 80,* 407–417.

Tuckman, J., & Connon, H. E. (1962). Attempted suicide in adolescents. *American Journal of Psychiatry, 119,* 228–232.

Van Houten, T., & Golenbiewski, G. (1978). *Adolescent life stress as a predictor of alcohol abuse and/or runaway behavior.* Washington, DC: National Youth Alternatives Project.

Walker, D. (1975). *Runaway youth: An annotated bibliography and literature overview.* Washington, DC: U.S. Department of Health, Education and Welfare.

Wallerstein, J. S., & Kelly, J. B. (1974). The effects of parental divorce: The adolescent experience. In E. J. Anthony & C. Koupernik (Eds.), *The child in his family: Children at psychiatric risk.* New York: John Wiley.

Wass, H. (1984). Concepts of death: A developmental perspective. In H. Wass & C. A. Corr (Eds.), *Childhood and death.* Washington, DC: Hemisphere.

Wass, H., & Cason, L. (1984). Fears and anxieties about death. In H. Wass & C. A. Corr (Eds.), *Childhood and death.* Washington, DC: Hemisphere.

Wegscheider, S. (1981). *Another chance: Hope and health for the alcoholic family.* Palo Alto, CA: Science and Behavior Books.

Wilson, J. P. (1978). *Identity, ideology and crisis: The Vietnam veteran in transition* (2 vols.). Washington, DC: Disabled American Veterans.

Wolkind, S. N., & Rutter, M. (1973). Children who have been "in care": An epidemiological study. *Journal of Psychological Psychiatry, 14,* 97–105.

INDEX

THE ENABLER: When Helping Harms the Ones You Love
by Angelyn Miller

An enabler protects others from the consequences of their actions. Always helpful and self-denying, enablers hurt the very people they love. They come between them and life and keep them from growing. As this book shows, enabling is a tragic, ironic trap.

At the root of enabling is low self-esteem. Enablers need to feel needed, to have others dependent on them. It took a severe family crisis for Angelyn Miller, a loving wife and mother, to realize that her husband and son had become dependents. They could no longer function adequately without her. In THE ENABLER, Miller describes her successful struggle to change.

With personal worksheets and self-awareness exercises, THE ENABLER offers help to those seeking a way out. Miller also recommends group-based work, such as the Twelve-Step approach found in AA, Al-Anon, ACoA, and related organizations.

Soft Cover ... 144 pages ... $6.95

HELPING YOUR CHILD SUCCEED AFTER DIVORCE
by Florence Bienenfeld, Ph.D.

Divorce is difficult for adults, and it can be devastating for children involved. Research shows that the damage can take years to heal.

In her many years as a child custody mediator, Florence Bienenfeld has seen the tremendous effect on children of parents' attitudes towards each other.

To help those parents who understand the need to make the divorce time as safe as possible for their children, Dr. Bienenfeld offers practical advice and guidelines on:

- Creating a "conflict-free" environment in which the child can feel loved by both parents.
- Making the transition from marriage partners to "parent partners" who are no longer married.
- Dealing with holidays, birthdays, and vacations.
- Using mediation to resolve difficult custody issues.

The book includes lists of child custody mediators and helping organizations nationwide.

Soft Cover ... 224 pages ... Illustrated ... $9.95

To order, please see last page

ORDER FORM

NAME

ADDRESS

CITY   STATE

ZIP   COUNTRY

TITLE	QTY	PRICE	TOTAL
The Enabler		@ $6.95	
Helping Your Child Succeed After Divorce		@ $9.95	
Couples in Collusion		@ $11.95	
Dynamics of Couples Therapy		@ $11.95	
Getting High in Natural Ways		@ $6.95	
Healthy Aging		@ $17.95	
Healthy Aging *(paperback)*		@ $11.95	
Not Another Diet Book		@ $15.95	
Once A Month		@ $8.45	
PMS: A Guide for Young Women		@ $6.95	
Raising Each Other		@ $7.95	
Trauma in the Lives of Children		@ $22.95	
Trauma in the Lives of Children *(paperback)*		@ $12.95	

Shipping costs:
First book: $2.00
  ($3.00 for Canada)
Each additional
book: $.50 ($.75
  for Canada)
For UPS rates and
bulk orders call us
at (714) 624-2277

TOTAL	
Less discount @_____%	(_____)
TOTAL COST OF BOOKS	
Calif. residents add sales tax	
Shipping & handling	
TOTAL ENCLOSED	
Please pay in U.S. funds only	

❑ Check   ❑ Money Order

Complete and mail to:

Hunter House Inc., Publishers

PO Box 847, Claremont, CA 91711

❑ Check here to receive our book catalog